COMMUNITY IN THE INVENTIVE AGE

COMMUNITY IN THE **INVENTIVE AGE**

DOUG PAGITT

Abingdon Press

Nashville

COMMUNITY IN THE INVENTIVE AGE
Copyright © 2014 by Doug Pagitt
Reprinted and published by Abingdon Press
First published by Sparkhouse Press

This book is printed on acid-free paper.

Library of Congress Cataloging-in-Publication Data has been requested.

ISBN 978-1-6308-8083-5

14 15 16 17 18 19 20 21 22 23—10 9 8 7 6 5 4 3 2 1
MANUFACTURED IN THE UNITED STATES OF AMERICA

CONTENTS

CHAPTER 1
THE INVENTIVE AGE

In 2003 I wrote about the holistic, missional Christian community called Solomon's Porch where I am a pastor. At the time, the church was three years old. Now, in 2011, the church is eleven years old. We've changed quite a bit since 2003, and like a house that's starting to show its age, this book needed a bit of a remodel.

A few years ago, Shelley, my wife, and I remodeled the kitchen of our 110-year-old house. The purpose of the remodel was not just to make the kitchen look different; it was to give us a new way of living in our house.

Our house was built in Minnesota toward the end of the Agrarian Age. While the official paperwork on the house dates it at 1930, I discovered it was actually built in the late 1890s. As I opened the walls in preparation for the remodel of the kitchen, I found newspapers used for insulation that were dated 1897. So either the builders of the house were quite the pack rats and hoarded newspapers for 30 years, or the house was redated when our part of town was officially incorporated in 1930. I chose to believe the latter.

In the one hundred-plus years since our house was built, the way people use a kitchen has changed. Back then, there was likely only one person doing the cooking, so the folks building the house didn't worry about making space for multiple people to work in the kitchen at the same time. Back then, they didn't have appliances that sat on the counter. They didn't have recycling bins. They didn't have snack drawers or dishwashers or giant upright refrigerators and therefore didn't need the space those things require. We wanted to be able to eat in our kitchen, something unheard of in the late nineteenth and early twentieth centuries—that's what the dining room was for. So we remodeled the house to fit the way we live in it.

After several months of upheaval, we had a "new" kitchen. But it wasn't entirely new. The walls are the same walls and one of the windows is from the original kitchen. It's in the same location relative to the family room and dining room. So it's a mix of what was there before and what needed to change to reflect the way we live in our house.

This book is a bit like our kitchen—a refreshed version of what was there alongside new ideas that make it a bit more inhabitable.

In part, the remodeling of this book is due to the way our community has changed since the book was first published. But it's also due to the way the culture in which our church exists has changed. When we started Solomon's Porch, we had just entered a new millennium. What we didn't know is that we had also entered a new era, one I have come to call the Inventive Age.

If you've come to this book having read my most recent book, *Church in the Inventive Age*, then you already know what that term means. If you're new to the phrase, let me give you a quick overview.

For most of human history, changes in broad social structures came occasionally and were limited in geographic scope. But in the last two centuries, cultural change has become far-reaching, constant, and increasingly rapid.

In the last two hundred years, American culture has moved through three distinct ages—the Agrarian Age, the Industrial Age, and the Information Age—and is heavily engaged in a fourth—an era I have dubbed the Inventive Age. With each of these ages has come a shift in what we think, what we value, what we do, and how we do it.

I was once in a small group meeting with famed organizational expert Peter Drucker. Out of everything he said at that meeting, one thought has stuck with me more than the others. He said, "The world my parents were born into was essentially the same as the world of Abraham and Sarah from the Bible."

He was, of course, right. Drucker, born in Vienna in 1909, was pointing out that the world into which his parents were born—specifically Austria in the nineteenth century—operated under a social structure that had been in place in rural areas for a millennium. He contrasted that with the world into which he was born—Austria at the dawn of the Industrial Revolution. Just one generation earlier, the majority of human beings lived like their parents and grandparents and great-grandparents had. They worked the land, rarely lived more than one hundred miles from where they were born, and knew they'd be lucky to see their fiftieth birthdays. Mid-nineteenth-century culture was, as Drucker said, nearly identical to the culture of the ancient Israelites. Both were part of the Agrarian Age.

The Industrial Revolution of the late 1800s brought about dramatic cultural upheaval in Europe and the United States. Certainly earlier inventions like the printing press had a broad impact on society. But the printing press didn't directly change the way people fed themselves or

moved from place to place or earned a living. The Industrial Revolution did.

People moved from farms to cities. Men and wom-
en who had once worked alongside each other in the fields
left their families at home to work in factories. Manufactured goods became the currency of the culture.

The next cultural shift began while the Industrial
Age was still booming. During the 1920s and '30s, the
Information Age began to take hold, thanks in no small
part to the growth of the manufacturing and shipping
industries that had taken place during the Industrial Age.
As people had access to books, newspapers, radios, and
eventually televisions, knowledge and information became
the most valuable assets of the culture.

In the same way, the Inventive Age is being born
out of the Information Age. Knowledge is no longer the
goal, but the means by which we accomplish new—even
unimagined—goals.

Few cultural institutions have been able to move
through all of these shifts with their central identity intact.
The church has been a steady—though not unchanged—
presence in each age. It has remained when so many other
cultural institutions have either fallen away completely
or morphed so cleanly that they no longer resemble their
former selves. I believe that's because the church has been
both shaped by and a shaper of culture.

There are people who hate the idea that the culture
impacts the church. They like to think of the church as a
bastion of stability in a sea of turmoil. They want to believe
that the church has somehow maintained a pristine, un-
touched essence even as the muck of society has swirled
around it.

That's simply not the case.

This isn't an insult to the church. The church ought to place itself squarely in the midst of a culture. Everything from the kinds of buildings we call churches to the way we expect our pastors to preach, our theology to be laid out, and our furniture to be arranged is meant to communicate something to the culture in which a church functions. I think that's good news.

As American society has moved from the Agrarian Age through the Industrial Age into the Information Age and now on to the Inventive Age, the church has moved right along with it. In each age, the church has adopted new values (the small, rural communities of the Agrarian Age gave birth to the parish model of church), new beliefs (the growing literacy of the Industrial Age changed beliefs about who could and should read the Bible), new aesthetics (the Information Age gave us education wings and Sunday School curriculum), and new tools (microphones and song lyrics on the big screen are products of the Inventive Age) that reflect the changes in the culture in which it exists.

HERE WE ARE, IN THE THICK OF THE INVENTIVE AGE.

It's an age when we have no idea what's coming next or where it will come from—and for many of us, it's thrilling.

Much of what we knew for certain fifteen, even ten years ago—that you needed a cable coming into your house to make phone calls, that a car could only run on gas, that once you started wearing glasses you had to wear them for life—has been turned upside down.

Right now, we live in a world filled with ideas and tools and discoveries we couldn't have imagined twenty years ago. There is bioengineered corn growing in the African desert. You can carry a library's worth of books in your hand and your entire CD collection in your pocket. Scientists can create entirely new materials at the sub-atomic level. You can get a college degree from your living room. There are people living in a space station. What's more, I can talk to them through my Twitter account!

In 1963 the U.S. Patent and Trademark Office processed 90,982 applications. In 2008 it processed 485,312. While the U.S. population doubled in that time, patent applications have increased more than five times.

But the Inventive Age isn't solely about inventions any more that the Agrarian Age was solely about farming. As in the previous ages, the Inventive Age is marked by changes in the way we think, what we value, what we do, and how we do it.

In every sphere of society—the hard sciences, social sciences, art, sports, music, health, technology, economics, transportation, communication—there is a level of creativity that surpasses even the Industrial Age for its impact on the culture.

That creativity has altered the way we think about ourselves. Children, young adults, and even older folks no longer wonder what they will be when they grow up. Now we ask, What do I want to do with my life? How do I want to spend my time? What can I contribute? These aren't questions about vocation. They are questions about impact, about meaning. We sense that there is no end to the options and that the future is ours to make.

The Inventive Age is one in which inclusion, participation, collaboration, and beauty are essential values. The values of the previous ages still exist, but in different, even subservient, roles. Knowledge is important, but only as a means to discovering something else. Repeatability matters but only as it relates to advancing an idea. Survival, however, is barely on the radar of most Americans; where nature was once a major threat, it is now something we have tamed and used and manipulated so heavily that there are cultural movements designed to save it. Not long ago, humanity feared the earth. Now we fear for the earth.

This is the age of Pandora, where I tell an online radio station what to play. It is the age of the App Store, where a major corporation hands control over to an open-source network of ordinary people. It is the age of Wikipedia, where anyone can decide what a word or concept or cultural touchstone means. It is the age when a bunch of college kids create a social network and seven years later it has more than 500 million users.

It is the age of ownership and customization and user-created content.

The impetus behind all of this personalization is not narcissism. It's the longing to attach meaning to experiences. People in the Inventive Age are looking for a sense of ownership, not of things or even ideas, but of our lives. We are keenly aware of our global community and how interconnected our lives are with the lives of people all over the world.

That sense of global community can be overwhelming. We want both to create our own place in that community and to contribute to its vitality. We don't want to simply use resources created by and controlled by others. As a result, there is a shift in the seat of authority. It isn't in the wisdom of the village leaders or the deep pockets of the factory owners or the knowledge of the corporate executives. Authority is found in the way our experiences come together and create reality. It is found in

relationships. We tend to be suspicious of objectivity, un-
certain if it is possible or even desirable. Instead, we give
great credence to authenticity, to context. Authority—as
much as anything else in the Inventive Age—is user
generated.

The implications for the church are just beginning
to emerge. In the last ten years or so, the values of the
Inventive Age—the drive to create, the search for meaning,
the sense of ownership, the open-source mentality that
pushes the Inventive Age ever faster into the future—have
scattered across the landscape of American Christianity
like seeds in the wind.

How they will take root remains to be seen. What
is clear is that just as the previous ages created the norms
of the church in their day, so it will be in the Inventive Age.
And just as church leaders in those ages asked difficult
questions about change, so it will be up to you to decide
how you will be the church in this age.

That's where this book comes in. Solomon's Porch
is a church of the Inventive Age. As I look back over our
last eleven years, I see the ways that our values as a community reflect the values of the Inventive Age. The ways
we have changed over these eleven years have echoed the
ways in which our culture has changed in that time.

This hasn't really been intentional on our part—
it's just what happens when Inventive Age people start a
church. But we have found much that is life-giving about
being the church in the Inventive Age and we want to
share that with other communities.

It's far too early to know where all of this will lead—
there are churches all over the world working on their
experiments in being the church in the Inventive Age and
there's no telling what will take hold and what won't. To be

sure, churches in the Inventive Age will have our share of mistaken notions, questionable practices, and bad ideas. But right now, at the dawning of a new age, it all feels like a beautiful revolution.

CHAPTER 2
575 WEEKS

January 2, 2000, seems like a lifetime ago. Or at least 575 weeks ago.

575 weeks ago, I started sharing the dream of what I thought Solomon's Porch could be.

575 weeks ago, we were graciously invested in by the Evangelical Covenant Church of America to help us get off the ground financially.

575 weeks ago, we signed a lease on a rented office space above a tea shop and Chinese restaurant in the Linden Hills neighborhood of Minneapolis. A lease that was only made possible with the forbearance of rent for six months as we did the repairs and remodeling that were necessary for us to meet in the 1200-square-foot space that became home for the next two years.

575 weeks later, I am watching our Sunday night gathering on my computer from Marco Island, Florida.

575 weeks ago, this kind of thing was impossible. Not only did we not have the technology to send out a live stream for people to watch on a laptop or a yet-to-be-invented iPhone, but we didn't know such a thing was

11

possible. Now I have the gall to complain about the poor quality of the video feed.

I realize that compared to denominations that have existed since the 1870s or 1530s, we are in our infancy. Compared to churches like Saint James Episcopal in Lancaster, Pennsylvania, where several of their charter members also signed the Declaration of Independence, we are just getting started. But for us, these 575 weeks have been a full and beautiful life.

THE NEXT 575

On the 575th night of Solomon's Porch, I am at the home of my dear friends Brian and Grace McLaren watching the live stream of our Sunday night gathering. Tony Jones, a Covenant Participant in our community, is leading the sermon discussion with "our" Rabbi, Joseph Eidelheidt. I call Joseph our "church Rabbi," but most importantly he is my friend. He used to be the Rabbi at a mega-gogue (think mega-church but for synagogues) in Minneapolis but walked away from it seven years ago to pursue a life with more balance. He now directs the religion program at Saint Cloud State University in Minnesota and stops by Solomon's Porch now and then to visit or participate in the sermon. Recently he started a Thursday night Torah teaching at Solomon's Porch for people from his community and ours. We are a Christian community, he is Jewish. He has things to teach us and us him.

I am quite sure that 575 weeks ago I would not have felt so at ease with a Rabbi teaching the Torah in our building on Thursday nights, let alone coleading the sermon while I was out of town. But now I see his participation in our community as being exactly what we had hoped for back in January 2000.

When I first became a Christian at the age of sixteen, I understood the story of God as the call to full participation with our world, and I dreamed of a church that lived out the story of God. I saw God collaborating with humanity from the start of the story: "So God created human beings in his own image, in the image of God he created them; male and female he created them" (Genesis 1:27).

I BELIEVED HUMAN BEINGS WERE CALLED TO LIVE LIVES THAT ARE INTEGRATED WITH GOD AND EACH ANOTHER AS ONE HUMAN FAMILY.

I saw Jesus calling his disciples to share in the authority that was given to him. I saw the story of God taking place on an intimate, first-name-basis level. To me, faith was personal and took place in particular places and times.

At the same time, I saw it as a faith that mattered not only to us as individuals but to all of God's creation. I saw it as a call allowing all to follow God in the way of Jesus and take responsibility for the faith we profess. I saw it as a faith that came to life through communities and a faith that changed as new people joined the promise. I saw it as a faith where there was always room for "the other" and the resources of God were shared and never hoarded.

I saw it that way in 1983. I saw it that way in 2000. And I see it that way today. What's changed in those years is not my belief in that faith, but my sense of how the church can live out an open-sourced, participatory, here-and-now kind of Christianity. I am grateful to be part of a community of faith that is living out that kind of faith.

And that seems like something worth at least another 575 weeks.

575 weeks ago, I hadn't coined the phrase the Inventive Age. But I had longed for a church built around a different set of cultural assumptions than those that seemed to drive the culture of churches I'd been a part of in the past. I knew that the practices and impulses have served previous ages well, but they didn't work for me or many of the people I knew.

At the same time, we worked very hard in those early conversations to make sure we weren't just react- ing to what we'd experienced but rather following the lead of those who had created the expressions of church we'd known. We didn't want to undo anything. We wanted to do something. We asked ourselves, What was the best thing about the traditions we came from? What was meaningful? Why was it meaningful? What could a church look like if it was a mix of the best of what came before and the hope of what could be?

We didn't have a clear picture of what that would be. That turned out to be the best situation possible. By not having an answer at the ready we were forced to create a community first and pursue answers down the road. It turns out that was very "Inventive Age" of us.

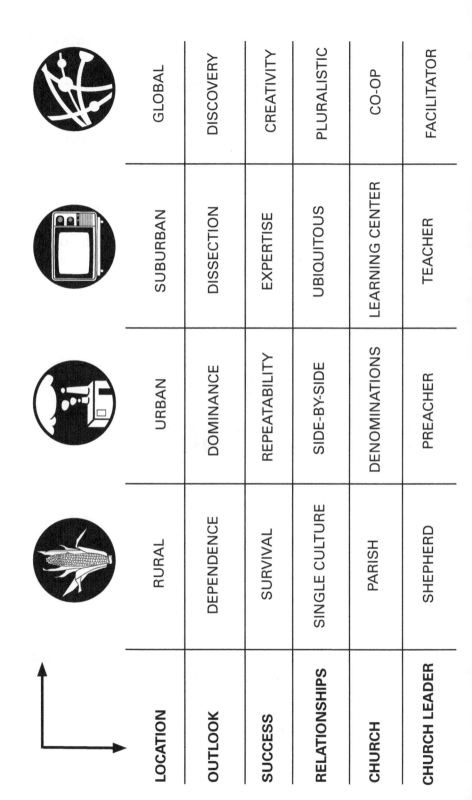

LOCATION	RURAL	URBAN	SUBURBAN	GLOBAL
OUTLOOK	DEPENDENCE	DOMINANCE	DISSECTION	DISCOVERY
SUCCESS	SURVIVAL	REPEATABILITY	EXPERTISE	CREATIVITY
RELATIONSHIPS	SINGLE CULTURE	SIDE-BY-SIDE	UBIQUITOUS	PLURALISTIC
CHURCH	PARISH	DENOMINATIONS	LEARNING CENTER	CO-OP
CHURCH LEADER	SHEPHERD	PREACHER	TEACHER	FACILITATOR

THE INVENTIVE AGE CHURCH

We had all come from Industrial Age and Information Age churches. And at the core of our longings was a sense that we were different people living in a different time from the people who had created those churches. We realized, at least intuitively, that the organizational structures that had held our religious experience were themselves cultural artifacts. We didn't want to sit still and sit straight. We wanted to relate to religious authority as peer, not as parishioner. We needed to organize in a new way in order to make change.

I have a confession to make, one that puts me in rare company in the professional ministry world:

I love being part of my church. I truly believe I have received far more from this community in the last decade than I could ever give to it.

I LOVE MY CHURCH.

I know many in the clergy serve their congregations as an act of commitment and chosen obligation. Their experience is one of struggle and sacrifice. For them it is a calling, and I honor their work. But that is not my situation. I would be part of Solomon's Porch whether I was paid my part-time salary or not.

I know that Solomon's Porch is not a perfect church—that's what makes it perfect for me. I know that not all churches can or should be like Solomon's Porch—the world needs all kinds of churches. But I also know that if there were not a church like Solomon's Porch, I might not be part of a church at all.

As we laid out a vision for the community we would become, we had a number of characteristics that kept rising to the surface. We wanted the church to be easy to access. We wanted everyone who entered our doors to feel included and invited to participate in the life of the community. We wanted to be a place where art and creativity and aesthetics mattered. We hoped to create a community in which people would be encouraged to live as whole people for whom faith was something lived out in every part of their lives.

These hopes influenced everything about the church we created. They came to bear on our thoughts about how we would meet, where we would search for truth, where we would locate authority. They played out in our decision to meet in the round and sit on couches. In other words, they influenced our community's values, our beliefs, our aesthetics, and our tools.

In recasting this book to reflect who we have become in the eight years since our story was first published, I began to see that those early hopes fall into ten broad categories that have shaped who we are:

MEANING MAKING

COMMUNITY FORMATION

RELATIONAL AUTHORITY

PARTICIPATION

COLLABORATION

ABUNDANCE

OPEN-SOURCE BELIEF

CREATIVITY AND BEAUTY

INTEGRATION

RESPONSIBILITY AND OWNERSHIP

These categories will serve as the spinal column of the rest of this book. They aren't the full picture of who we are, but they are the pieces that connect and support us.

In the coming chapters, I will show you what life in our community looks like. I'll be telling you about the room we meet in and some of the ways we live out the values and beliefs of our community, but the room we meet in and the things we do are only important as the artifacts of the people in our community. Certainly it matters what we do, for all communities are created by their practices, but we are first and foremost a people.

What shapes us are the people sitting on our couches, the people writing our music, the people spending time with our children. These people shape and form me. They shape and form each other.

Because of this, there are values in Solomon's Porch that won't exist in other communities. They didn't exist in our community until the people who brought them to us came along. Every community is shaped by the people in it, so what works for us might not work in your setting. Our failures might be smashingly successful in your community. So rather than looking for principles that will apply in every setting, I encourage you to notice ideas and impulses. See how they function in a unique context and find the patterns that arise. Consider how these characteristics of the Inventive Age might play out in your place and time.

CHAPTER 3
MEANING MAKING

Our attempt at being a church began in January 2000 in a small second-floor loft space in a hip little neighborhood of Minneapolis called Linden Hills. The church was birthed from conversations between a few friends who shared a desire to be part of a community of faith that not only had a new way of functioning, but generated a different out-come. At that point I had said, on more than one occasion, that I didn't think I would be able to stay Christian in any useful sense over the next fifty years if I continued with the expression of Christianity I was currently living—pretty disconcerting stuff for a pastor.

This was not a crisis of faith in the typical sense; I never doubted God, Jesus, or my faith. And yet I had a deep sense, which has actually grown deeper since, that I needed to move into a Christianity that somehow fit better with the world and not an expression reconstituted from another time.

My religious training and experience is from the evangelical stream of Christianity. I came to Christian faith as a high school junior from a background with absolutely no religious experience. I was immediately a leader within a campus high school ministry. I began attending churches right from the start, was engaged in ministry and Christian

witness from the very beginning. Within a decade I was
a seminary graduate, had ten years of wonderful experiences as a youth pastor at a nationally recognized mega-
church, and was a frequent speaker at regional and national youth events.

My world wasn't crashing down, I wasn't at a moral
crossroads, I hadn't hit rock bottom. There was no big
dramatic shift in my thinking, but rather this lurking sense
that there were levels of faith I knew nothing of and yet
needed to enter if I was to remain a Christian at all. It was
a feeling I couldn't shake, and yet I also felt like I couldn't
fully articulate what I needed. I just knew I needed something to change.

When I shared this nagging sense of discontent
with a few others, I found them feeling a similar desire
for expressions of faith built around new forms and new
outcomes. Together, we decided to try to organize our lives
around a way of living life in harmony with God. (While
this might sound very grandiose, it was really more of
a pathetic, groping attempt, not to discover something
beyond Christianity, but to live in the very Christianity we
were captured by in the first place.)

I have no regrets over my experience within the
evangelical faith community. I will always be grateful to
the institutions and people who invested so much in me,
yet my life experiences have led me to desire ways of
Christianity beyond the practices and beliefs of my beginning. My experience as an evangelical was a great place
for me to start, but not a sufficient place for me to finish.
Solomon's Porch was fueled by a desire to find a new way
of life with Jesus, in community with others, that honored
my past and moved boldly into the Inventive Age.

I now understand that most of my frustration
stemmed from evangelicalism being a product of the
Information Age. As a person with Inventive Age sensibili-

ties, I felt a deep sense of misalignment between how I experienced the world and how the church explained those experiences to me.

A BENEFIT AND A BLESSING TO ALL THE WORLD

In the circles I ran in back in the late '90s, short summations of Christianity were very much in vogue. One of the most common was "Christianity is not a religion, but a relationship with God." There was something appealing about this kind of tidy definition that was meant to make faith more than a meaningless ritual. But over time it began feeling like code for allowing my life to be limited to self-indulgent efforts centered on a personal experience with God with little regard for faith's public usefulness to others.

I began asking questions of my life and faith that were not centered on how deep my faith was but how useful my life was in bringing about the things of the kingdom of God. Being a properly trained evangelical, I paid great attention to the Bible and the call of faith it entailed. So I began looking through the Bible to find the impetus for a life that was good for the entire world.

Much of the thinking behind Solomon's Porch—and hence this book—came from those years of inquiry. A particular phrase from the book of James was especially meaningful: "Religion that God our Father accepts as pure and faultless is this: to look after orphans and widows in their distress and to keep oneself from being polluted by the world" (James 1:27).

As we started forming the practices that would become Solomon's Porch, this idea helped to set us on a path of being people who are concerned with more than our own salvation, but with practicing a Christian faith that is useful in the world.

Over the years, we started using a phrase that has served as a kind of charge for our community:

"TO BE A BENEFIT AND BLESSING TO ALL THE WORLD."

This great little phrase reminds us that we exist for this world and not just the next.

BEING THE BLESSING

In February of 2011, we held our annual Covenant Participant meeting. Like most churches, we use this time to review the previous year and look ahead to what's next. As part of this meeting, we had asked the facilitators of each of our nine working groups to talk briefly about what these groups were up to. It was among the best thirty minutes of my year.

Let me give you a little background on these groups. About three years ago, we decided to completely reconfigure the way we make decisions in our community. When we started in 2000, we set up something we called a Leadership Co-op. This small group was designated as the decision-making body for the church. For reasons I'll get into later, this plan proved to be less-than-ideal. So in 2007, the Leadership Co-op spent a weekend at the farm of a family in our community. Together, we dismantled the structure of our community and disbanded the Co-op. It was a great weekend.

We decided that instead of eight people holding the decision-making power, we needed to spread it out to the rest of the community. We looked at what was going on at Solomon's Porch and decided there were about twelve categories of activity—art, missions, our gatherings, administration, facility oversight, hospitality, music, children and families, that kind of thing. Instead of the eight of us thinking about all of these things, we asked the people who were passionate about those parts of our life together to create groups that would dream about and facilitate these activities.

In the three years since we made this change, these groups have morphed a bit, but the meeting in February was a clear demonstration of how right we were to spread the leadership of our community to as many people as possible.

Jessie talked about the Community Care group that coordinates meals for families with new babies or people recovering from an illness. They send care packages to our college students and organize the Easter Brunch. They connect newly married couples with older couples in our community for support and mentoring.

Adam, who facilitates our Tapestry Groups (these are small, task-oriented groups made up of Covenant Participants) talked about new ideas for helping these groups function more effectively. Paul, who is a relatively new Covenant Participant and new to the Administrative Working Group, talked about the upcoming budget process and the ideas his group has for helping us stay on track. Carla told us about our various Artists in Residence—a songwriter, a video archivist, a neighborhood liaison, a health-care practitioner—and announced an art and music event that will take place in the fall.

We heard about the great work going on with our kids, the many changes we are making to our aging building, and our ongoing commitment to our friends in Guatemala. All of this is happening because people in our church are committed to being a benefit and a blessing to all the world.

From the beginning, our desire has been to step into the present with a grateful attitude toward the past and to generate a way of life that's sustainable for the future.

WE HONOR THE REFORMERS, OF ALL AGES, BY DOING WHAT THEY DID AND NOT JUST REPEATING WHAT THEY SAID.

There is a need for us to be people who are always re-forming, as it were, to be constantly seeking to create new ways of life and new ideas about theology, service, and love that is fitting for our world and our time.

I recognize that today's "post" is tomorrow's "passé," and I'm okay with that. We are called to make our contributions in the world as a blessing for those we live with and for those who follow, but we are not mandated to create the processes and patterns of the future. While future generations will contend with the history we leave them, we need not create "the thing" for all ages. I certainly don't think the reformers intended for their ideas about the church to be its final form for all time. And I certainly don't want my children to be burdened with an expression of faith that fit for my time but not for theirs.

My hope is that what we do today at Solomon's Porch will inspire future generations to dream their own dreams and give life to their own visions rather than feeling the pressure to implement ours.

At the end of each chapter I will include the lyrics from one of the many "homemade" songs of our community. You can access the recorded versions of these songs and find others on our website at www.SolomonsPorch. com/Music.

LET THERE BE PEACE

Let there be peace
For the children of war
For those who will fight
For those who will die

Let there be love
For the women on sale
For those who will cry
For those all alone

Let there be hope
For the man who got broke
For those who lost trust
And then lost themselves

Let there be love
That we're guilty of
Let there be hope
For the weak and the poor
Let there be peace
For the us and the them
Let there be peace
For the me and the you

Let there be peace
For the us and the them
Let there be peace
For the me and the you

—Javier Sampedro

CHAPTER 4
COMMUNITY FORMATION

Here in the Inventive Age, the formation of meaningful community is more than a strategy, more than a means to some other end. Community in the Inventive Age is an end in and of itself.

This is a significant shift from previous ages. For example, in the Agrarian Age community was a given. People lived near essentially the same group of people for most of their lives. They shared a language, customs, and resources, and this proximity and linguistic harmony created community. But in the Inventive Age, community is created in the midst of a pluralistic engagement of people from many backgrounds and experiences. Most of us find that our best friends grew up in other towns, had different experiences, and often had different goals in life. Commonality has been replaced by distinction.

In the Industrial Age, the workplace replaced the hometown. Common practices and language grew not out of a shared background but out of a shared commitment to a common purpose. But in the urban, multi-connectional Inventive Age of multiple jobs the workplace doesn't create a sufficient level of connection. For most people, the place you work has only a minor impact on your sense of identity and community.

The Inventive Age has created a need for what sociologist Ray Oldenburg calls the "Third Place." Identity doesn't come from the family or the job, but from a self-selected place of connectivity and engagement.

I am writing this chapter in a coffee shop and I can overhear the conversation of two women in their early 70s. One just told the other that her life has changed dramatically in the last five years. She had recently moved for the first time since 1981. Her husband had died and she was talking about her need to develop new relationships. She said, "With most of my family gone or living in other places, I connect with people at the airport where I volunteer, in my sewing club, and sometimes still at church. I'm discovering a whole new me."

THE INVENTIVE AGE IS NOT ONLY EXPERIENCED BY THE YOUNG.

I don't think there's a church around right now that doesn't use the word community as a kind of buzzword. Large churches use it to make sure people know they won't get lost in the crowd. Small churches use it to emphasis their intimacy. Churches of all shapes and sizes use it to signal their involvements outside of the walls of their buildings. It can mean people who live on the same street, or people of a similar ethnic background, or people who think the same way about issues. In our current vocabulary, community can mean everything and nothing at the same time.

We use that word at Solomon's Porch as well. We call ourselves a "Holistic Missional Christian Community."

In the hopes that the word community can retain some meaning for us, we think of it through four lenses: Local, Global, Historical, and Futurical.

By local community, we mean the people in our physical proximity—those we live by, work with, drive past, and stand next to in line. It includes those we recognize and those we don't. It includes those who are like us and those who are not.

While the concept of local community certainly includes the churches in which we worship, I find that for many Christians their fellow congregants play no more crucial a role in their lives than the people they walk past in the grocery store. They share a common experience from time to time and receive services from the same organization, but little else. In order for community to mean something in our context, the people of Solomon's Porch are finding ways to make our community of faith a place where we become involved in one another's lives in intimate, meaningful, transformative ways.

This kind of intimacy requires us to move beyond simple accountability and instead calls us to vulnerability. Accountability is built on the notion that each of us will do our own work as we seek to live Christian lives and that others do what they can to keep us on track. But we want relationships where we don't merely ask others to hold us to living in the way of Jesus, but where we invite them to participate in our efforts to do so.

WE'RE TRYING TO OPEN UP OUR LIVES IN SUCH A WAY THAT OTHERS DON'T JUST KEEP US ON TRACK, BUT BECOME ACTUAL AGENTS OF OUR REDEMPTION AND CHANGE.

We also understand ourselves as part of a global community. As Christians, we are called to live our local expressions of Christianity in harmony with people around the world. The beliefs and practices of our Western Church should never override or negate the equally valid and righteous expressions of faith lived by Christians around the world. At Solomon's Porch we're seeking to be aware of the ways in which our version of Christianity is culturally derived and make ourselves open to God's work in the global community of faith.

Christian community also includes those who have lived out the faith before us, our historical community. Just as with local and global communities, there are elements of our historical community that can be difficult to live with, elements we could never see ourselves replicating (the Crusades, supporting the slave industry, the Salem Witch Trials, etc.). At the same time, it's through our historical community that we are reminded, guided, taught, and led in the ways of God. We are compelled to enter into the context of those who have served, loved, and believed before us. Our current and future vision for the church cannot be formed without a sense of the visions of the past.

When we were starting our community, we knew our understanding of community couldn't just end there. We felt ourselves called to live in community with those who come after us as well. They are the futurical community.

The word itself came out of a discussion of part of the Bible that I no longer recall. But one of the people in that group, a twenty-year-old named Luke, said that we needed to always be aware of the legacy we are leaving for those who follow us. He said, "What would you call it? Futurical?" And we have ever since.

While the people of Solomon's Porch are seeking to create expressions of faith that are meaningful for us in this time and place, we are also striving to grow into people who will bless future generations and guide them to do the same for their time and place. We are living the history of the generations that will follow us.

There is something compelling, powerful, and liberating about living life in harmony with God, not in the isolation of an individual relationship but as part of a community that includes those around us, those far from us, those who came before us, and those who will come after us. At the center of this holistic, communal approach to spiritual formation is the creation of Christian communities that are a continuation of the story of God, from Abraham to Jesus to today.

What you will find in the rest of this book is our desire to live in an Inventive Age community.

SING IT BACK TO ME

I know a few things
But I don't know if I'm reaching you
Yes I know so many things
They've all got pieces of you and me

So we will go on
We sang it in a song once

Will you sing it back to me
Wrap it back around me
Sing it back to me
I need to know it surrounds me

'Cause I know a few things
But I hope this one is blessing you

And we will go on
We'll sing it in a song now

Will you sing it back to me
Wrap it back around me
Sing it back to me
I need to know it surrounds me

—Ben Johnson

CHAPTER 5
RELATIONAL AUTHORITY

One of the curses of being a pastor of a new church is the need to justify the existence of our community. I wish I could count the times that I was asked by insiders of Christianity, "So who are you targeting? What demographic market are you going after?" I usually attempt to divert this kind of conversation by saying something like, "Well, that's not really how we approach this." But what I'm really thinking is that targeting is something that tobacco companies and snipers do, and that the one who is targeted rarely appreciates it.

We didn't start Solomon's Porch with the idea that we had a corner on the market of God nor that we had a product of faith that we could deliver more effectively than other churches. As odd as it sounds, the efforts of Solomon's Porch began as—and remain—our attempt to be people of useful faith. We never intended Solomon's Porch to be specially formulated to meet the needs of Generation Whatever. Sure, we're a young community—although we're not as young as we once were—but our attention isn't focused on a demographic approach of meeting the felt needs of a particular generation.

We are not interested in living a fulfilled version of our current lives. We are seeking to become something else, something more.

The commodification of Christianity might be among the greatest threats to living a viable Christian faith that we face in our world. There is a need to seriously rethink the idea that everything, including Christianity, is a product that can be marketed, sold, and consumed to meet needs. Unfortunately, much more energy has gone into discovering the best use of marketing techniques for the church than reflecting on what happens to the gospel when it becomes a product of an ever-desiring culture.

Our practices are genuine expressions of our collective community, not marketing tricks. At first glance, some of our ways might seem trendy and many of them have and will continue to change as our community changes, but we are not trying to be culturally chic. We are trying to live a life that is candid and authentic.

It's not just Christians who ask what we're doing. During the early days of Solomon's Porch, there were times when people would walk by our space and notice us working.

"What are you doing?" they'd ask.

"Well, we're starting a church," I'd say, secretly hoping they'd ask when they could start coming.

Instead, the typical response was, "Starting a church? What are you doing that for? Aren't there enough churches already?"

Now that is the kind of interaction that can take the wind right out of any upbeat church starter. Finding a legitimate response for those questions—not to mention my own conscience—became serious business.

After months of discussing the integrity of our intentions as a group, we realized that we started Solomon's Porch not because the pews in other churches were full, but because the places of dream making and leadership in other churches were full. We all felt that there were too few places where those who are envisioning new ways of Christianity could birth those dreams in existing communities of faith.

Our desire was not to create a place where outsiders would simply hear the truth about God in attractive and relevant ways, but a place where we would all experience the transformative workings of God through community. This kind of lengthy convoluted explanation may not have been sufficient for the cynic on the street, but sure proved useful for us to understand who we were becoming.

ANY TIME A CULTURE SHIFTS FROM ONE EPOCH TO ANOTHER, A QUESTION IS RAISED: WHO'S IN CHARGE?

My friend Phyllis Tickle puts it this way: "In this changing culture we must constantly ask, 'Where does authority now reside?'"

The usual places of authority have lost their prestige in the Inventive Age. The structures of authority—governments, denominations, military forces—may still exist, but the actual power has shifted. In the church, we no longer grant authority just because someone has gone through a process of ordination. The ecumenical movements of the last fifty years have allowed people to see denominational systems as options, not authorities. Nor is it enough to have a seminary degree. Degrees are commonplace and most every church has a few seminary grads sitting in the pews (or couches). And it's not enough to know more than the congregation. With literacy rates sitting around ninety percent and easy access to libraries and the Internet, knowledge is cheap.

AUTHORITY IN THE INVENTIVE AGE COMES THROUGH RELATIONSHIPS.

It is granted from the community, not bestowed by outsiders. Authority still exists, but its origins have changed.

We see this in technology and social media. In social marketing, people are more interested in the reviews and recommendations of their friends than of experts. There's a saying common in youth ministry circles that goes, "Kids don't care how much you know until they know how much you care." This gets at the heart of relational authority—we grant it to those with whom we have a relationship.

We think of Solomon's Porch as a family. Not one with a mom and a dad and a few kids, but a big broad, adoptive, changing family. It's a family where people are marrying in and dying off, where siblings and half siblings who might not ever know one another let alone feel connected to each other in meaningful ways if not for the family, where the distinction of blood lines are irrelevant.

My wife and I have four children. Only two of them carry our genetic make-up. The other two are brothers who joined our family by way of adoption through the foster care system in Minnesota. I realized the other day that of the five other people living in my house, I'm only biologically related to two of them. I picked the other three. But there's no difference in the connection I have with my biological son and daughter and the relationships I have chosen with Shelley, Ruben, and Chico. We are all bound by our relationship to one another.

When we started our community there was no Facebook or Twitter. You couldn't "Like" a video on YouTube and have it show up on your friends' feeds. Simply put, there was no social media.

But instinctively, we were creating our own social network—that's what churches have always been. Long before people created networks with digitally coded 1s and 0s on portable devices, we sought out and created communities in which we could find our identity, collaborate, and participate.

THE NETWORK

What makes a church like Solomon's Porch a different kind of social network than the churches of the Agrarian, Industrial, or Information Ages is that we have organized ourselves around a different kind of networking system.

Every collection of people is organized around one of three systems:

- Bounded Set

- Center Set

- Relational Set

Each of these sets is important and each serves a particular function. Every church falls into one of these systems, either by design or by default. These systems help organizations figure out everything from who makes decisions to how events take place to who can participate in the community. We'll take a brief look at each system as a way of understanding what makes a place like Solomon's Porch an Inventive Age church.

Bounded Set

In a playground, the fence serves as the boundary. Children can play safely in the playground because the fence differentiates the safe area from the street. The problem is that too often the fence becomes the point of focus. Those who study children's behavior on playgrounds note that when children are on playgrounds with a fence, they spend a significant amount of time hanging on the fence, sticking arms and legs through the fence, kicking balls over the fence. Any system that uses the bounded-set theory knows the work that goes into preserving the boundaries.

Bounded-set organizations have definable rules: in and out, right and wrong, member and nonmember. These are very important organizational patterns. They provide safety, connectedness, familiarity. People in bounded sets know what's expected of them.

There are plenty of great reasons to hold to a

bounded set. Certain organizations are based on the idea that there are rules for entrance and maintenance of membership. If everyone could be part of the group, the group wouldn't have any identity. The rules can come in many forms—ethnicity, belief, finances, family connections, education, profession, adherence to a set of ideals or commitments. Fraternities, civic groups, sports teams—they are all bounded sets that depend on there being some separation between those in the group and those outside of it.

There are some who prefer their faith to be organized by bounded-set organizational theory. They want there to be a line of some sort—baptism, a confession of belief, a particular doctrinal position—that people have to cross in order to be part of the faith. Some churches prefer bounded-set theory because it helps define participation—only certain people can perform particular tasks. It helps everyone understand who does what.

Bounded-set churches were the norm in the Industrial Age. In the Agrarian Age, churches were organized by location—you attended the church that was closest to your farm. But as people moved into the cities and churches popped up on every corner, it became increasingly important for churches to distinguish themselves. So it mattered that this church had infant baptism and that one didn't. It mattered which church had an ordained preacher and which one didn't. These boundaries of doctrine and belief and practice became central to how Christians understood themselves and their communities.

Center Set

While the bounded set works very well for some organizations, it isn't the best fit for others. For some, boundaries feel like arbitrary restrictions that limit access to the faith. They are more comfortable with a system that does not require adherence to a collection of rules or edicts as a prerequisite for participation.

Instead, they suggest there ought to be only a few key issues for the community to gather around. The center set shifts the focus from the things that keep people out to the things that bring people together. The center might be a topic, an issue, a belief, or a practice.

If we go back to the playground analogy, the center set is the playground with all the equipment smack-dab in the middle of the park. The kids are so drawn to the center that there's no need for a fence. The center keeps them where they need to be.

The center-set way of thinking about faith and church participation has been freeing for many people. They don't like the implications of the rule-based form of religion that goes with bounded-set faith. It feels exclusive and legalistic. So they are drawn to the idea that people can gather around a positive expression of faith rather than an "us and them" paradigm.

The center-set approach is ideal for the Information Age. Many Information Age churches and organizations have built community around common statements, understandings, and beliefs. They hold the perspective that the closer they are to the core, the closer they are to one another.

When information is king, then getting the words right is crucial. So many center-set churches will spend a great deal of time refining the words used in their worship services. The meaning of those words is not to open new possibilities but is meant to stay rock solid in order to limit the distance someone might drift. In this context, tools like a statement of faith are not the beginning of conversation. They are the punctuation.

While those who hold to a center-set system would

have a hard time recognizing it, the fact is that the center set really isn't all that different from a bounded set. The only real difference is that there are fewer "essentials" in the center set. But if those essentials are called into question, the response is surprisingly similar to the responses of the bounded set.

I was talking with a friend of mine about this. He mentioned that he is no longer a bounded-set adherent when it comes to his views of Christianity. "I used to believe that people had to believe a long list of doctrines, stop doing certain practices, and start doing others before they could be part of the faith," he said. "But I've left all that behind. Now I believe that there are only three things that are essential to the faith." I responded with two questions: "How did you decide which three to keep?" and "Doesn't it feel better to only have three and not the long list?"

In answer to the first question, he just nodded with that assured look as if to say, "You know, the really important ones," as though any reasonable person would know what those are.

He responded to the second question by saying, "Oh, way better. It's so much more true to the spirit of Jesus and his teachings!"

I smiled at him and said, "If you think going from a long list to three felt good, just wait until you go from three to zero!"

And then he was silent. It was clear he had no interest in a faith that did not have a set of predetermined essentials. Or, to say it more accurately, he couldn't conceive of a faith without mandates.

When you have predetermined requirements for

participating in a community, it makes little difference if you've got a wall's worth or just a few to gather around. They serve the same function—to determine who is in and who is out.

Relational Set

If the bounded-set playground has a fence and the center-set playground has a premade play area, then the relational set is like a self-organized playgroup where each parent brings a bag of toys for all the kids to share.

A RELATIONAL-SET SYSTEM IS ONE IN WHICH THE PARTICIPANTS ARE THE ORGANIZATION.

The playground fence and the equipment exist whether anyone is there to use them or not. But the play-group doesn't exist until the kids show up.

Where bounded- and center-set organizations are fixed—the boundaries and the center rarely change—relational sets are fluid because they change as the people in them change. Everyone in the relational-set organization has the power to shape the system simply by being in it.

Most of us experience all kinds of relational-set organizations in our daily lives. In fact, the relational set is far more common than bounded or center sets. From the interaction of molecules, to the gravitational pull of the

BOUNDED **SET**

CENTER **SET**

RELATIONAL **SET**

earth on the moon, we can see that living in dynamic inter-play is the organizing principle of creation.

The Internet is another obvious example of a relational-set system. There is no boundary to the Internet, nor is there a center. It is made up of interconnected hard drives, software, routers, switches, and gateways. The Internet gets its power from the people who create it.

We also see it in our families. A family can rarely exist as a bounded-set organization. Sooner or later some-one falls in love and marries the outsider. Or a child has a personality that breaks all the rules. Or a long-lost relative is discovered and the bubble is broken.

A center-set family is equally impossible. The "es-sentials" would change with each marriage, each genera-tion, each child. Think of immigrant families. Even the expectation of a common language often only lasts one generation. Traditions change as new people enter the family or elders die or family members move.

A family is a relational-set system, so much so that some of us have to attend family reunions with a score-card to keep track of who had a baby and who adopted a child and who got married and who got divorced. The system changes as the people in it change.

No one would argue that the family is a weaker system because it is a relational-set system. We know instinctively that a relational-set organization is the most powerful, integrated, and sustainable of all types.

STRUCTURING A RELATIONAL SET

The success of a person's work life in the Inventive Age is often dictated more by her personal and profes-sional network than by her schooling or education. In the last twenty years, there has been an explosion of network-ing organizations and tools to help people find and change jobs. A career change is not accomplished by retooling but by reconnecting. This is because the Inventive Age is about who you know and not what you know. It is a relational age.

It used to be that Ivy League schools were valued because the best and smartest people taught there. But the success of the Information Age created more and more highly educated students and educators. Now, the qual-ity of teaching at small colleges, state, and community colleges is on par with the elite schools of previous ages. Schools market not only on the professors but on the alumni. It is not just about what students learn, but the contacts they make.

While relational-set systems are powerful, they are also complicated, particularly when there are decisions to be made. Let me give you an analogy to show you how complex that process can be.

The human foot has twenty-six bones (that's a quarter of the bones in the body). It has thirty-three joints; more than one hundred muscles, tendons, and ligaments; and a network of blood vessels, nerves, skin, and soft tissue.

Every time a person takes a step, a complex inter-action takes place not only in the foot but in that person's whole body. A foot is a small foundation for a human body to stand on. What makes upright walking possible is not the size of the foundation of the foot, but the flexibility and interaction of the foot with the rest of the body as it works to maintain balance and propel itself forward. With each step, the foot must respond to the rest of the body. Walk-ing, let alone running and jumping, is tricky business.

When we started Solomon's Porch, we knew we wanted to be a relational-set system. And when there were eight of us in that system, it was pretty easy for everyone to have a say and for our "foot" to work efficiently.

It didn't take long for our forward movement to become much more complicated. As other people joined in on what we were creating, we quickly saw the challenges of staying relational. We knew we needed to adapt and create a way of managing our organization.

I love this kind of stuff. I love thinking about structures and systems and organizational theories. When we started thinking about the best way to organize ourselves as a church, I came to that conversation with a good understanding of our organizational options. So I made a suggestion. I thought it was a great idea and so did other people. But, as it turns out that suggested model was a mistake.

We decided to put together a Leadership Co-op. This model was based on my experience as our local non-profit co-op grocery store where shoppers were members of the co-op. The members would select a dozen or so people to serve on a board that would lead the store. This was attractive to us as a way to move beyond a consumer/provider model to something of a community activity.

In our minds it had all the marks of a solid relational-set system. The Co-op would be made up of six to ten people who would think about the strategic and financial issues of our growing organization on behalf of the whole community. I asked a handful of people to consider being part of this group and most of them said yes. The problem was that the people I asked were the people who were the most heavily involved in our community at the time.

I know that sounds like the perfect group of people to ask, but there were two reasons why it didn't work:

1) These people were passionate about the community, but they were not necessarily interested in the tasks of the Leadership Co-op. Just because people are active and involved in a system doesn't mean they want to run it. We violated a rule we now work hard to hold to—people should only be asked to lead things they care about.

2) The Co-op had such a broad array of duties there was no way all of us could care about all of them. We were asking one group of people to make decisions about staffing, about budget issues, about our building, about giving, about our community involvements, about pastoral care issues, and all the other odds and ends that come with running a church. It's just not possible for people to stay committed to caring about all of that for the long run.

As a result, the Co-op felt like a burden to all us, right from the start. Eventually, that group sat down and dismantled itself.

In the last few years, we have transitioned to a completely different relational-set structure. This time, we are working off of the idea that we need leaders, but the same leaders don't lead everything. People lead what they are passionate about leading and nothing else. People who care about how we nurture the faith of our children lead us in that area of our life together. People who really love to crunch numbers do that. People who love to think about how we create our Sunday night gatherings do that. We see all of these groups as interconnected, but they are led by different people based on their interests and passions. Everyone is invited to lead in the areas that are life-giving for them.

The system is also based on the assumption that everything matters equally. There are not more urgent matters than others. It matters what happens with our money and budget, but it also matters what happens in our Sunday night gatherings and what happens with art and with the meals we serve to the working poor and the AIDS hospice in our neighborhood. These elements of our life together flourish because they are not in competition with each other. In the Co-op days, the six or eight of us could only tackle so much at a time. Now, there are more than one hundred people involved in making all of this happen.

WE'VE ALSO FOUND THAT OUR SYSTEM WORKS BEST WHEN THERE ARE NO RESTRICTIONS ON WHO CAN LEAD.

It's often people who are new to our community who introduce us to new opportunities. It's not unusual for someone to join in on the Tuesday Sermon Discussion Group just days after coming to her first Sunday night gathering. Someone showing up for the first time on a Sunday might be handed a plate of bread and a stack of cups and asked to help set up for communion.

We assume people are capable just as they are. They don't need an upgrade or some kind of training to lead us. Who they are is enough. Even those who struggle with mental health (and we have many of these folks) or those who are experiencing instability in their lives are encouraged to lead and guide and participate in whatever ways they want to. When they do, they are joining in with others who share their passions and who are eager to bring them along in the life of our community.

When I talk about this, someone almost always asks about safety. They want to know how we keep our community safe in the midst of this kind of openness. I know they worry that we have crazy people teaching our children or thieves counting the offering money. But we believe that being open is the best protection. Trouble comes when systems are closed and power sits in the hands of the few. I have never heard of a manipulative cultic group based on radical openness and participation. But I know of plenty who have at their core privacy, leadership levels, and a special clergy category. It's hard to keep secrets in a community in which life is shared openly. We have come to believe that "many eyes" serve to protect.

THE PLACE OF THE PASTOR

For churches, discussions about relational-set systems leave one glaring elephant in the room: What happens to the pastor? It's obvious where the pastor fits in to the bounded- and center-set systems, but where does the pastor fit in the relational set? More to the point, where does the pastor's authority fit?

I've had to come to terms with that question as well, not for my own sake, but because so many people have expectations of what a pastor does and how that role functions in a community. The more I've thought about it, the more I've come to see that the role of pastor carries far more cultural implications than theological implications.

There is a cultural understanding that the person who has a seminary degree and leads the sermon most of the time is the pastor. There's an expectation that this person is a mash-up of CEO, therapist, motivational speaker, and biblical scholar. There are pastors who want to be all of those things and who work hard to fulfill those cultural expectations. I'm not one of them. Instead, I want to help people consider the role of a pastor in a different way.

In our setting, we don't have a designation for clergy. I don't have special privileges that come with my paid position as pastor.

EVERYONE IN THE COMMUNITY HAS THE SAME ACCESS TO PEOPLE AND IDEAS AND PROCESSES AS I DO.

My personality is such that I can sometimes be more vocal or involved in some of those things than other people, but that's because of my nature, not my job title.

While we believe that everyone is equal in all things and all roles are equally valuable, there are always personal preferences that cause people to hold some roles in higher esteem than others. I happen to place far more value on the visual artists and musicians in our community than I do the sermon givers. My wife believes that those who spend time with the youngest members of our community hold the most important role. We all have our preferences and ideas about who is the most important person in the community and we are careful not to force people to assume it's the pastor.

I know that no matter how much I say that I am no different than anyone else in the church, there will be those who, by nature of my job title, believe I am the leader of the community. So I do what I can to keep directing the authority those good people give me back out into the community. If someone wants premarital counseling, I send them to one of the many married couples in our community who are ready and willing to meet with engaged couples. If someone wants to talk about giving money to the church, I send them to one of the people who works with our budget. If someone has a concern about the sermon, they are invited to join us on Tuesday nights to talk through the Bible with other people from our community. If someone's friend is getting married and looking for an officiant, we give them a license to perform the ceremony.

In the previous cultural ages, the role of the pastor may well have been to be the teacher, or the caregiver, or the denominational brand. But for me, my role of being the pastor is to be a facilitator of our common experiences. This includes the experiences of the faith in the past and the faith of the people in our community and around the world. In many ways my role is to curate spaces where we can learn, live, and make a faith that can hold up in the Inventive Age.

HOPE OUT LOUD

In this frozen town are you broken down
Have you found your way around here?
Run your daring dreams aground here?
You've settled down
Jesus newly form your beauty
Heavenly surround
Breathe in story
Sing out glory
We're gracefully allowed.

What we hold to now
Is that we hope out-loud
It takes a crowd to figure how near
The Lord God moves around here
Round and round

Jesus newly form your beauty
Heavenly surround

Breathe in story sing out glory gracefully allowed.

What we hold to now
Is that we hope out-loud
It takes a crowd to figure how

What we hold to now
Is that we hope out-loud
It takes a crowd to figure how

Jesus newly form your beauty
Heavenly surround

—Ben Johnson

CHAPTER 6
PARTICIPATION

At the time I'm writing this chapter, the dominant international news stories are the democracy protests in Egypt, Tunisia, Libya, Bahrain, and other countries. It is not clear as to what the future of any of these movements will be, but what is clear is that the early twenty-first century is a time of participation across the world.

In many ways this is not fueled by outreach efforts of the world's other democracies (in fact, in many of these places the United States has helped to support the former regimes). These latest democracy movements are fueled by people demanding to participate in their future.

The era of the dictator is coming to an end. The Internet and social media are fueling this participation movement. When people know more and are better equipped, they start demanding a greater role in their own affairs.

The Inventive Age rewards and encourages participation, but participatory culture is not clean or easy. There are tremendous difficulties embedded in this approach, and the outcomes are not guaranteed. Still, participatory culture is the expectation for Inventive Age people.

Our way of valuing participation at Solomon's Porch

is to function more like a jazz band than an orchestra. We aren't really interested in having every person in the community play off the same sheet music. Instead, we ask everyone to bring their instrument and play along in a kind of extended jam session.

Tim Lyles is part of our community at Solomon's Porch. He's also a professional musician and music instructor. I asked him to share his insights on improvisation in jazz music. Not surprisingly, there are important parallels for churches in the Inventive Age. Here's what he had to say:

To the uninitiated listener jazz music often gives the impression that anything goes, chaos is the rule, and performers are playing any random thing that pops into their heads. This misguided impression comes from being exposed to only the simplest, sugar-coated music: music that deals in mostly the two basic tonalities [major and minor], melodies that stay contained within the "do re mi" scale, and rhythms that are so primal that there can be no mistake where the "1...2...3...4" is. Simple is good, and there is some jazz that covers that base nicely, but jazz music is expansive and moves beyond simple idioms.

Jazz music is most commonly typecast by only one characteristic: improvisation. A lot is made of this aspect, but that emphasis can cause people to overlook the other elements that typify jazz. That's not to say improvisation is not an important element of jazz. Improvisation in jazz means injecting a personal interpretation into an old "standard" tune of the musical canon or even an original piece and using the internal structure of the chord changes over which solos are taken by members of the band.

Of course a musician has to be a very strong technical player before he or she can improvise well. Improvising a solo means stepping out into thin air without having much preknowledge of what is about to be played. There is typically a deep knowledge of the chords and form of a piece [numbers of measures, repeated phrases] nurtured by years of melodic and motific conditioning, but specifically what will unfold in a solo is a mystery to all involved.

Jazz players place great emphasis on being able to read music accurately, being able to navigate complex chord changes, knowing internally a large repertoire of hundreds of standard tunes, and being able to instantly transpose them into any key and interpret them in a variety of styles. Other styles of popular music put great emphasis on the song itself: the melody and lyrics, the meaning of the words and what emotions they invoke. An instrumental solo is merely a diversion in the arrangement. In jazz it's often the other way around. The song is often merely a vehicle for the performer's interpretation. After the melody and form of a song have been stated, the solos are typically the centerpiece, the meat of the expression, before the melody is restated and the arrangement ends.

When not soloing, musicians are judged by their ability to support the solo, to anticipate where it's going, and to complement it. There is a skeletal structure being followed, but there is great liberty for all instrumentalists within that structure. This lends itself to a conversational quality as the performers interact. The soloist can influence the accompanists and vice versa.

For the audience, even those who don't know all that much about music, there is an implicit recognition when a soloist is playing it safe by using a vocabulary of familiar licks and patterns and a visceral thrill when a soloist is exploring unfamiliar territory.

THE CASTLE ON THE CORNER

Our community is currently housed in what was formerly Hobart United Methodist Church in the Kingfield neighborhood of Minneapolis. This is our fourth neighborhood and third semi-permanent location. We never meant to be a community on the move, but that's how our history has played out.

We started in a 1200-square-foot loft space in a neighborhood about a mile west of our current location. After two and a half years there, we moved six miles east to a highly socially serviced neighborhood where we stayed for three and a half years. Our 4,000-square-foot building served us well, and we would have stayed had the property not been sold to a group who turned it into an Islamic mosque and community center for the Somali community in the neighborhood. That move came about quickly, and we ended up sharing a space with a generous Presbyterian church in the LynLake area of Minneapolis while we looked for a place of our own. It felt a little like moving into your parents' basement after living on your own for several years. We were grateful for the space, but itching to have a more permanent home.

After six months, we began to lease our current space from the Methodist denomination. The congregation of Hobart had dismantled and the building was being used for various lessees. The Methodists needed an anchor tenant and we needed a home. We hope to be here for a long time.

Moving has taken a toll on us because relationships are so important. Each time we have moved, we have seen changes in our relationships. While each move has given us new connection and neighbors, it has also left others to wither. We have committed each time to not let this happen, but the realities of location are much greater than our intentions. Not only are the relationships we've left behind daunting, but having to form the new relationships and practices can suck the wind out of you as well.

It can seem incongruous to some people that a church like ours that bears few of the outside marks of a typical "church" meets in a building that looks like a classic Industrial Age church. We are the castle on the corner: brick walls, a bell tower, no parking, steps leading up to carved wooden doors. It is a fortress.

I might be the only person at Solomon's Porch who is bothered by meeting in a church building, particularly one that bears the marks of an age in which churches were meant to look like factories and functioned much like them as well, building faith through the denominational structure in which consistency and sameness were valued.

I don't like that keeping our old boiler running takes up a huge portion of our budget for six months of the year. It bothers me that the building is not only hard to manage for those in wheelchairs or who have trouble managing steps, but that making it more accessible is prohibitively expensive for us. I am not thrilled that our building is the tallest and most ominous structure on the block. I like a building, and a faith, that live more commonly in the neighborhood, that keep a lower profile.

I wrestle with having a building that communicates that rising above the ground is a necessary part of connecting with God.

But I am in the minority with this view and this 17,000-square-foot building is home.

We can't do much about the outside of our building, but we have worked hard to make the inside feel like us. You can't get two feet inside the building before the décor reinterprets the English castle feel of the outside.

Just inside the front door, there is an artisan shop with goods created by people of Solomon's Porch—books, paintings, jewelry, note cards, mittens, photographs. It is less of a church bookstore and more of a craft fair.

Continuing up the stairs, the original plaque of Psalm 23 is the last comforting item for those looking for the normal church trappings.

Taking a left into the Gathering Room creates a bit of pause for some people. Often on Sunday nights, I watch people walk in the Gathering Room and I can tell the first-timers pretty easily. They usually pause just inside the door. I can understand why. They aren't sure where to go. There's no center aisle, no discernable "front" or "back" of the room, no clear path to a seat. If they aren't greeted by one of our friendly folks—and they often are—it takes them a moment to get their bearings. The other week was a classic. Over the course of the night I saw seven people come in for the first time. They all paused. Three smiled. They had that "Well isn't this something?" smirk. Two looked surprised. Two put their eyes down as they hunted for the first seat they could find.

It might be the splash of color that gets them. The combination of mustard yellow walls, colorful stained glass windows, the collection of multi-patterned couches from the 1970s, the tongue-and-groove wood ceiling that the previous congregation installed in the mid-'80s, and artwork on the wall will not win us any design integration awards. But the room has a warm humility to it. There are large projector screens on the side walls so that people can sit anywhere and see them clearly. Our musicians are tucked into one corner, right around where people might expect a lectern or a baptismal font. The raised area that was once the nave of the church now holds several couches, small café tables, and space for toddlers to roam around.

The furniture is set up in the round, so as people stand in the doorway, they see the backs of as many couches as fronts. And at the center of the room, next to a large round coffee table and surrounded by couches, are two barstools that will be used by several of the people participating in the gathering. The person making the announcements will sit there, the person leading the sermon time will sit there, and sometimes a preschooler will wander up and take a spin.

The far side of the room opens into another comfortable space. We call it our Family Room, and on a Sunday night, it is as lively as the Gathering Room. Filled with food, art, and conversation, this room is often the victor in the battle for hearts and minds and attention spans of our people.

As people wander through the rest of the building, they notice that every room is a different color. When we moved in, all the walls were white—every wall in every room and every hallway. In our warehouse space, we'd painted every surface we could find, marking it as ours in some primal way. We'd spent six months living in someone else's "house" and we were eager to mark our new home as a symbol of our reclaimed independence.

We opened up the painting process to the community, asking people to choose a room or a hall or a closet and paint it. There was no master plan to the color scheme of the building. People who had adjoining spaces might consult each other, but it was essentially a free-for-all. Within a week of moving in, we had nearly every room— including the three-story sanctuary—painted. Now we have a golden Gathering Room and a sage green Family Room. Our hallway is bright orange and the basement is sky blue. It's a vibrant, lively space and true reflection of the people who created it.

I tell you all of this not because I think you need to paint your walls, but because our building is a big clue for the people who enter it. This place is made up of the people in it. It's our artwork, our paint choices, our furniture that surrounds us. It is a space put together through the collaborative, participatory efforts of our community.

WORSHIP AS PARTICIPATION

The value we put on participation can be found in every element of our lives together. It is perhaps most obvious in our Sunday night gatherings.

We have gone back and forth on the issue of having one or two gatherings, and while most of us prefer to have one, the logistics of space and comfort have led us to go with two. So we have gatherings at 5 p.m. and 7 p.m. on Sundays.

People are sometimes puzzled when the music doesn't start until ten minutes after the hour. At least once a month someone asks me, "Why do we start late?" I tell them we aren't starting late,

WE'RE STARTING WITH CONVERSATION.

That's important because this conversation is the heart of who we are. Our hope is that the music, the call and response, the prayers, the sermon, and family-style communion that follow will be a continuation of the conversation.

We originally called these "worship gatherings," but over the years we realized how that language made it seem like worship only happened during that Sunday night event. This gathering is crucial to our life together and acts like a family dinner where we touch base with each other, share an experience, and bless each other as we move into a new week. But it's not more important than other meetings that happen in the community. We feel like everything we do as a community—from our Wednesday morning playgroup to our Tuesday night Sermon Discussion Group—is worship. We now call this our Sunday night gathering.

This becomes clear during the lengthy announcements on Sunday nights. We work hard to make the rhythms and opportunities of our community accessible for everyone, no matter how long they've been part of Solomon's Porch. So we take time to explain the regular happenings.

We also have an open announcement time in which anyone can let us know about some event or opportunity. Sometimes it's a birthday party. Sometimes it's a job opening. Sometimes it's a request for prayer. I think the open nature of the announcements is one of the more important elements of our Sunday nights. It communicates that this place belongs to all of us. It says that the meals we have, or the serving we will do, or the need someone has for help matter to all of us. They are as important as the sermon, songs, and communion.

Because our Sunday gatherings are designed to be interactive and participatory, our furniture is set in the round so we can see one another. This helps us engage one another during the music, prayer, and discussion times. Admittedly, this has been a stretch for us Minnesotans who don't like to draw attention to ourselves. But over time, we've gotten used to seeing faces in church rather than the backs of heads.

We have chosen to not use the concert metaphor for our worship. Since the 1880s, one of the dominant metaphors for church structures has been the theatre. In the 1960s, this evolved to the concert setting, a stage-focused environment with performers on one level and the audience on another. The use of stages, lighting, and electric sound reinforcement of music and voice has become so commonplace in most churches that most of us never question why it's there.

While this format is familiar and works well for the communication of a single message to large settings of people, it also has a limiting effect as people try to engage collectively in communal worship. Attention is directed toward the stage and the words coming from it. The relationship is between the audience member and the speaker, not between fellow audience members.

We had a few choices of the kind of seating we could pursue for our worship gatherings: the pew, the "theater" seat, and the couch. Each one brings with it the expectation of a particular outcome. The theater seat invokes a feeling of wanting to be entertained. The pew brings anticipation of a lecture. The couch brings about notions of home. You can probably guess why we chose the couch.

Part of our communal effort on Sunday nights is to limit the things that separate those in charge from those who are not. That's why it's important that the roles people play not be confused with power in other areas of our community. We don't have special places of activity, or certain rights that are reserved for only some (well, we do have gender specific restrooms). Because we don't have a stage, we don't have to be concerned with who is utilizing that place of power. As I mentioned earlier, the stool in the center of our gathering space is used by a variety of people during the gathering. The stool, which is as close as we get to a pulpit, is open to all.

For the same reason, we have resisted the use of microphones. Microphones give undue power to the people using them and suggest they have the authority to speak to the entire group in ways others do not. We are conscious of the feelings that come when one person has the ability to address the crowd with sophisticated sound reinforcement and what that communicates to others about whose words are important.

Again, logistics sometimes trump our desires, so we do have some sound reinforcement. Our musicians have microphones on stands and we have three small hanging mics over the center of the room so that whoever is speaking in that space—giving announcements, inviting us to communion, leading the sermon—can be heard in the room. But people also speak from where they are sitting. They make an announcement, they offer a comment on the sermon, they chime in on the welcome or share a bit of news. It's clear that you don't have to have access to a microphone to be heard in this community.

Since the beginning of Solomon's Porch, we have done things in particular, and often peculiar, ways. But we have tried not to be peculiar for the sake of novelty.

WE ARE MORE INTERESTED IN CREATING AUTHENTIC PRACTICES THAN UNUSUAL OR TRENDY PRACTICES.

When making decisions about what we will do, we regularly ask the questions, "Does this fit us?" and "Are we acting in a natural way?" more often than "Is this something that will attract new people?" Authenticity is more valuable to us than slick production or professional execution.

We would prefer to have people speak, sing, and create with sincerity than with polish. We are haunted by the image of the falsely friendly sales clerk who calls strangers "honey," and acts like your best friend even as he swipes your credit card. We'd rather just act like us, and hope people are warmly greeted.

Our Sunday gatherings combine regular elements with occasional surprises. While special inclusions are always welcome and add variety, it is in the routine practices that we find our rhythm for living.

MUSIC

The music we use in our gatherings is a home-grown expression of our faith. We have a disproportionate number of talented musicians who write and perform our music. They have created—and continue to add to—a repertoire of songs we rotate through so we're able to bring both freshness and familiarity to our singing.

In our community, the style of music extends beyond mere praise and worship. Our songs serve to instruct, to teach, to call, to plead, and to express; music is narrative, it's prayer, it's a physical discipline. Some songs are meant to be sung by all and others are meant to wash over us. Because our music is written by us, it is both personal and communal.

When our community joins together with those who have created the music, the words and melody come alive and dwell among us. So much of Christian expression is ethereal and conceptual, but singing songs written by our friends grounds our worship in the here and now. Ben, Corey, Javier, Sarah, Brooke, and others who write our music know the lives of their friends here, so when they write songs that plead for God to create something new in us, they are giving voice to the longings of our community.

Songs are not just words we sing; they are invitations into a way of life. Writing our own songs allows us to have an expression of faith that is true to us and our world. They give us a place to say, "This is what we believe. This is what we confess. These are not the words of others; they are in agreement with others but they are our songs."

Our music is certainly one of our most distinctive elements, so it garners a great deal of conversation and curiosity. I've found that people often assume we use our own music because we have something against the music of other churches or other generations. Anyone who tries to take us down that road doesn't understand in the least bit what we are doing. We use our own music precisely because we honor the music of our predecessors. Our desire is to make our contribution to the beautiful legacy of music in the church.

One of the roles of the church through the centuries has been to put faith into stories and songs that fit their day. This is what we're doing. Because we're committed to being a community that not only benefits from the church that has gone before it but also contributes to the church that will follow us, we want to do all we can to implore our in-house poets and musicians to create.

For us, music is not understood as preparation for learning, it is learning. It is not a precursor to worship, it is worship. It is more than a cognitive slide show of hopeful escapism. It's one way that we physically express our faith. For us, worship is not fanaticizing about somewhere else, but an attempt to create a place of physical participation in the life of God with our bodies, in a place, with a certain group of people and a very real God. In the Inventive Age, we are all equipped for engagement, even with the Holy.

STORY

During our Sunday gathering, there are a few times we all stand and say something in unison. On a normal night, one of those readings comes after the first song of the night. We stand together and read a call-and-response invocation. Most of the time this reading is led by a woman. This is an attempt to comment on the fact that far too often Christian worship is dominated by male voices. We have structured a practice that serves both as a reminder and balance.

We write these invocations ourselves and change the reading a few times during the year. This current version was inspired by a group of people who are looking at our financial life. They asked if they could infuse this part of the gatherings with some thoughts their group had put together. The reading is meant to remind us that we join together in spirit, time, and finances.

ONE: PEOPLE OF SOLOMON'S PORCH TONIGHT WE MEET

ALL: IN THIS PLACE BUT NOT LIMITED TO THIS PLACE,

ONE: WE DESIRE TO LIVE RIGHT WITH ONE ANOTHER

ALL: AND ALL THE WORLD

ONE: SO, WE COVENANT WITH ONE ANOTHER

ALL: TO NOT CONSUME ALL WE HAVE FOR OURSELVES

ONE: WE COMMIT OUR LIVES AND MONEY

ALL: TO THE EFFORTS OF GOD AND THOSE IN NEED ANYWHERE IN OUR WORLD

ONE: WE JOIN OUR RESOURCES AND LIVES TOGETHER

ALL: IN RESPONSE TO THE GENEROSITY OF GOD

ONE: YES, PEOPLE OF SOLOMON'S PORCH TONIGHT WE MEET

ALL: SEEKING TO BE OF BENEFIT AND BLESSING TO ALL THE WORLD

This invocation is one of the ways we tell our story each week. It reminds us of why we gather each week, of who we hope to become as a community, and of how we want to live in the world. It takes up less than a minute of our gathering time, but it sets the tone for the rest of our time together.

We tell our story in other ways as well. Nearly every week, someone from our community takes a seat on the center stool and tells us what they are up to in the world and how they are following God in the way of Jesus. We often have friends from other churches around the world visit us, and when they are around, we have them tell us their stories. We hear about budding communities in Guatemala or Australia, the work someone is doing in Haiti or California, the efforts to build wells in India or buy bikes for AIDS orphans in South Africa. We hear from the people in our community who work with at-risk teenagers, people who are recovering from broken marriages, people heading off to graduate school or camp ministries.

This storytelling is central to our lives together as we share our experiences, listen to the experiences of others, and allow the story of God to provide a better understanding of both.

When I say we share our stories, I don't mean that we give the classic church testimonies. Sometimes the stories have to do with faith, trust, God, and the particulars of Christianity, but not always. Sometimes people talk about issues that remain difficult for them to deal with. Sometimes they talk about their work or a ministry they're involved in. No matter what they talk about, we're careful not to make it part of some bigger agenda or try to use their story in a particular way. Doing so would mean these stories cease to be an open invitation into someone's life and become little more than sales pitches.

When people share their stories, they invite others into their lives. They open a part of themselves that otherwise could not be entered without permission. There is trust, vulnerability, and a posture of being focused on the other. Those who are listening sense a welcome to delve into their own stories, to make themselves vulnerable, to trust others with their pain. When they are shared, individual experiences become communal experiences. This is hospitality at its most profound.

COMMUNION

Our weekly gatherings also include communion. For us, the practice of communion has gone beyond a ritual and moved into the realm of necessity.

There are people in our community for whom communion is a kind of litmus test for how comfortable they will be in a church. Some come from backgrounds where communion is so steeped in ritual that, for them, it's lost all meaning. Others come from traditions where communion was an infrequent event or one that was seen primarily as a remembrance of an old Bible story. The experiences of all of these people have moved us to take great pains to make communion a time where we are not just looking back on an event, but also looking inward and looking forward.

We do communion "family-style" each week. A different person introduces communion from his or her perspective. We have a common reading we do as part of this introduction, but people are also invited to add whatever commentary they like to the introduction. Some will read from the Bible, some will talk about the communion traditions of churches they've been part of in the past. Some will talk about why communion is hard for them, others why it is meaningful for them. This gives communion a new practical and theological meaning each time.

I suppose this can give people a sense of theological whiplash week to week. And if that the person making the introduction was assumed to be the official spokesperson of the church, it would never work. Our hope is that these varied introductions are seen for what they are—an invitation to understand the experience of the one giving the instructions. Rather than worrying that the person is not offering the right explanation, we find ourselves discovering expanded ways of understanding communion.

Once the introduction has been made, everyone is invited to share the elements that have been set up around the room. We encourage people to break off chunks of bread and hand them to others, to pour cups of juice or wine and pass them around. Everyone has access to the elements. There aren't special people who give these ordinary elements meaning. We are ordinary people serving one another special elements. The bread is good quality and full of taste. Both juice and wine—good stuff, not the kind that leaves a coating on the bottle—are available in a common cup or individual cups.

The reading we do together in the midst of all this is something I wrote to encourage people to participate in the communion introduction. Some people don't like to stand up and talk about their experiences, so I wanted to give the less verbose among us a little cushion. It reads like this:

WE TAKE COMMUNION BY SERVING AND EATING BREAD AND WINE TOGETHER, IN COMMUNITY WITH FOLLOWERS OF JESUS AROUND THE WORLD AND THROUGHOUT ALL AGES. WE ENTER THIS MYSTERY PROCLAIMING AND HAVING FAITH OF JESUS AS THE MESSIAH, WHOSE LIFE, DEATH, BURIAL, RESURRECTION, ASCENSION AND SENDING SHOW THE LOVE OF GOD FOR THE WORLD, FREE US FROM SIN, AND INITIATE THE KINGDOM OF GOD IN OUR WORLD IN NEW WAYS, FOR THE BENEFIT AND BLESSING OF ALL CREATION.

This serves as a "best of" communion explanations introduction. We've adapted it a bit over the last few years, and I'm beginning to wonder if it has served its purpose. But for now, it creates a common experience and encourages participation.

SERMON

Most of our gatherings include a time when we engage with the Bible. Typically, we choose a book of the Bible and work through it by reading and discussing a chapter or two each week. It usually takes us several months to work through a whole book. (I will not spend much time discussing the philosophy and theory of preaching here, but you can find a full discussion of Progressional Implicatory Dialogical preaching in my book *Preaching in the Inventive Age*.)

The sermon basically consists of the community reading the chapters out loud—we project them on the screen and take turns reading—while the person facilitating the sermon provides a running commentary. Most of the time that person is me, but we have lots of other people who like to do this as well. This commentary includes historical clarification as well as reflections of what may be of consequence for our community.

The commentary is a group effort, having been shaped the previous Tuesday in our Sermon Discussion Group. That group, which is open to everyone, previews the reading for the coming Sunday and talks through its implications while we work to enter into what it has to say.

The Bible is our primary text for the sermon. I don't typically quote experts or other literary sources. I don't put together a three-point thesis or make a great effort to apply what we're reading to life today. Instead, we want to know the story of God and see our lives in relationship to what God is doing, has done, and promises to do.

ALLOWING THE BIBLE TO SPEAK FOR ITSELF IN LONG SEGMENTS HAS BEEN ONE OF THE MOST POWERFUL THINGS FOR ME.

Hearing it read in the voice and intonation of whoever the reader is for that slide has oftentimes added texture and even changed how I understand the text. There is little doubt that this style of communal sermon creation has changed me greatly. Our interactive dialogical approach has allowed me to not only deliver sermons most weeks, but to hear great ones as well.

Some sermons come in twenty-minute blocks and some in twenty-second comments. There have been so many times when a comment or question shared as part of the sermon has opened new vistas to me. After hearing the brilliant observations and ideas of people in our community, I see my job as creating a context where the hopes and dreams and thoughts and prayers of the people of our community can shine through. It has been a growing experience for me to see my role as a facilitator of conversation rather than the speechmaker. I was trained to give compelling speeches. But like so many in our community, I'm helped far more by engaged conversation than by even my best one-way communication.

Our hope for the sermon is that it allows us to find ourselves in that story, to see how others have played their part and be informed by the ways they followed God. Reading the Bible through this lens offers a tremendous perspective for those of us who tend to get stuck in the muck of today.

In what many people see as the most obviously participatory part of our gatherings, the sermon is followed by a time of open discussion with comments, interpretations, and thoughts of significance from our community. During these few minutes, not only are brilliant observations made, but people are reminded that we are called to listen to and be taught by one another.

The open invitation to participate in the sermon — both in its preparation and in the sermon itself — can make some folks nervous. They worry that someone will say something heretical, that some weird guy will make an inappropriate comment. But we value inclusion more than we value conformity. We want to hear from the weird guy. Sometimes we even let him preach the sermon.

CHILDREN

We love children at Solomon's Porch. Our intention on Sunday nights is to create an atmosphere that is conducive for children's spiritual formation. We want children — and their parents — to be full participants in the life of our community.

When we started Solomon's Porch, the only children joining us were mine. But over the past three years, the number of children has exploded. We're not just adding babies but elementary-aged children as well. When we started, we had a small playroom for babies and toddlers and planned simple art projects for the older children to work on at the front of the gathering space.

Our new space has provided us with the room to give our children more to do. During the sermon, our toddlers head to one of the rooms created just for them. There, they dance, listen to a Bible story, sing, or work on art projects. These youngest people of our community lead and teach the rest of us what it means to participate in the kingdom of God in the body and not be only concerned about what we learn in our heads.

Our elementary children are with us for most of the gathering, but when the sermon starts, they head into a room of their own where they spend time with the Bible in ways that are meaningful for their developmental stage. Both the elementary children and the preschoolers are making their way through an eight-year story arc that will introduce them to the whole narrative of the Bible. They spend a month on each Bible story, discovering it through stories, art, service projects, and movement.

One of the significant concerns we had in our early days as a community was that our children would be left in the dust as we blazed a new trail for our own spirituality. I remember on more than one occasion wondering if our four children would hit their adult years and say, "Mom and Dad, you know when we were doing that hippie-wannabe church thing? I didn't learn anything and I wish I had." I can happily say that the children of Solomon's Porch are experiencing an integrated, physical faith.

Our efforts with our children are not meant to lead them to a better cognitive understanding but to nurture the ways they experience God in their lives right now. It's our way of recognizing that they are no more required to have faith figured out than we are and that their process of following God in the way of Jesus will take a lifetime, not an hour. Our children might not know all the superstars of flannel-graph faith, but they are learning the ways of a holistic faith that ripples through every part of their lives.

We do not have an official nursery, but we do offer "baby holders" in the Gathering Room and safe spaces for babies to crawl and play in the midst of our gathering space. We remind parents and all of us to not be bothered by babies making a little noise or crying a bit. Crying babies remind us that it is good to take time to listen to one another cry—even during the "important" times of life.

Including children in our lives sends a message to their parents as well. It tells them that we want their presence and their voices with us, not off in some "crying room" or nursery where they have to stay separated from those of us who aren't lucky enough to have sweet babies to tend to. By asking them to stay even when their babies are a little fussy or nursing or crawling around the floor, we tell those parents that they are full participants in the life of our community.

We like to think of children not as somehow different from us, but as people just like us, simply younger (and much cuter). They are creators of our community. We are shaping them, but they also shape us.

This is a different message than what was communicated in Information Age churches. The Information Age tended to see children as vessels to be filled with knowledge and teaching. But in the Inventive Age, children are understood as being active learners and teachers. They are not just receptacles, they are generators.

We have a communal practice of welcoming children into our community. In some traditions, this is done through baptism. In others, through a prayer of dedication. In our community, we welcome both approaches but also offer an anointing with oil. The imagery of anointing is to see the physical presence of the blessing of God staying on and nourishing the child just as the oil does.

Often parents ask for their newborns to be introduced to the community and anointed. I have crafted a little blessing to go along with the placement of the oil.

Not long ago we welcomed little Asher into our community. While placing the oil on him, we prayed that Asher would have God's wisdom in his head, that his eyes would see God's glory, his ears hear God's call, his heart be God's home, his hands do God's work and his feet follow wherever God leads.

Just before the anointing, I asked the people of our community to stand and extend their hands, joining in the anointing. As they did, I noticed the eclectic outfits of a half dozen kids at our gathering. Jackson was wearing a bear mask and pajama bottoms, Charlotte wore a princess outfit with cowboy boots. There was a decked out Spider-man, four-year-old Ella sported face paint, and a toddler wearing hardly anything at all.

I had to say something.

I reminded our community that while we will inform and shape Asher, these other children remind us that he will be uniquely himself, just as they are themselves. He will have a way that might not be ours and will see a world that makes sense to him. We need him to show, lead, and teach us.

It might be a bit of an oversimplification to suggest that in the Industrial-Age church children were to be seen and not heard and that in the Information-Age church children were sent to special classrooms to be filled with truth. But it's clear that in the Inventive Age, children are seen as full participants in our churches who have the call and the opportunity to shape us—and our communities.

WE'RE NOT ALONE

We have arrived here in ways wide I know
Barely escaping from past-times, some untold.
We find ourselves about something, and together we have
shown
More than we expected; thankful we're not alone.

Peaceful God
Hopeful God
Somehow, always
We have known.
Twisted as life can be
Relentless complexity.

What time is this for me? I'm asking to hear.
A part of a history; a story so dear.
We are told of how to be a blessing undoing fear.
A Victorious living mystery, a people whose kingdom is
near.

Peaceful God
Hopeful God
Somehow, always
We have known.

We're not alone
The kingdom is near.
Living the mystery.
Undoing fear.

We're not alone
The kingdom is near.
Living the mystery.
Undoing fear.

—Ben Johnson

CHAPTER 7
COLLABORATION THROUGH DIALOGUE

It was a Tuesday night back in 2004 and I had just arrived at church for the Sermon Discussion Group. (I admit that for a church of pretty artistic people, we don't have very creative titles for our happenings. We kind of like simple, straightforward names for things). On Tuesday nights, a group meets from 7:30 p.m. to 9 p.m. to read and discuss the section of the Bible we'll be looking at during our Sunday gathering. When I arrived at the building, Kayla was waiting in her car and stepped out to meet me. Our attention quickly turned to the two young men who just pulled over to our side of the road. They were parked in the same place where two other guys had been selling drugs from their car a couple of weeks earlier, and it seemed to me their intentions were the same.

I let Kayla into the building and headed back outside to make eye contact and let our "visitors" know that this was a street where people pay attention. As I walked around our front "yard" picking up garbage and generally making my presence known, I couldn't help but wonder if what we were about to do in the Sermon Discussion Group had any real effect on that neighborhood.

At the time, we were meeting in an old warehouse in heart of the most socially serviced neighborhood in

Minneapolis. We were surrounded by the various plights that are part of poor neighborhoods all over the country. While I knew that our conversation that night would be of some use to those of who showed up, I wondered what use is was to people who are victims and perpetrators of the pain that comes from illegal drug use and the poverty that so easily condones and supports it.

These are the kinds of questions that dog me as a pastor and keep me constantly re-evaluating how we should go about living in the way of Jesus in our time and place. Seven years and two neighborhoods later, those questions still nag at me, as they should. When I stop wondering if the faith we're practicing is useful, I hope someone will take away my keys to the church and send me packing.

OPEN FORUM

The Inventive Age demands that we join together with all efforts of goodness in the world. It is not sufficient to pit one good thing against the other. We are compelled as proclaimers of the gospel to live a modern-day version of Jesus' call to recognize that "those who are not against us are for us." We are on the same side as anyone seeking to make the world a better place. We are not concerned about whether the church gets credit for that activity, nor do we concern ourselves with the motives of others. We see the outcomes as speaking for themselves.

The way we find connections to our fellow co-workers is through dialogue. But dialogue is often in short supply in our world. At Solomon's Porch, we are embracing the Inventive Age practice of engaging in dialogue, not simply finding those who agree with us. It's not easy but it's worth the effort.

Most Tuesday nights, the Sermon Discussion Group ranges in size anywhere from five to twenty people. As with all of our community activities, this discussion is open to everyone, and most nights are a mix of regulars and a few first-timers.

We begin the Sermon Discussion Group by having each person introduce themselves by sharing their full names—first, middle, and last. Everyone—regulars and newcomers—does this, and we do it every week. It partly serves to get people comfortable talking in this setting, but it also says something about us. The use of full names sends a message that we are more than our first names. The use of our middle and last names serves as a reminder that we come from families who gave us our names and have impacted us and shaped the people we are as well as the beliefs we hold. It also sets a framework for the coming discussion to be people-centered, rather than only idea-centered. This implores us to act with respect and dignity even when we do not care for someone's contributions.

Each week includes a time where everyone shares an answer to a light-hearted question, like what's your favorite candy or the name of your second-grade crush. These weird little tidbits go a long way toward helping us learn more about each other and seeing each other as complex human beings with a history of experiences. It's also a little hard to be too intimidated by someone who just told you she wishes she could still wear her moon boots. Most importantly, these questions get people used to talking in the group and to hearing their own voices holding center court.

We spend the next bit of time reading through the Bible text for the following Sunday. Each person reads until they want to stop, then the next person picks up the reading and we go on like that until we're done. We also try to read from a few different translations of the Bible so we get a broader, deeper understanding of the text. Sometimes we'll pull out the Greek lexicon to find the root of a word that's puzzling to us, but it usually doesn't help much; the English versions seem to do a more than adequate job for us. After we finish reading the whole thing, we talk about the issues raised, any confusing elements, and what it tells us about our role in God's story. The energy of the conversation moves from person to person as each one shares thoughts and ideas.

For some, this is sort of an upside-down way of looking at the Bible. It's more common for a pastor or an individual to approach the Bible with a subject in mind, and then search for what it has to say on that topic. But we've found it to be an amazing process to gather as a community and let the Bible unfold and lead us.

That doesn't mean we just open the Bible and pick a place to read. Rather, our intention is to allow the Bible to function as a full member of our community where we listen to the Bible on every subject of which it speaks. This setting allows the Bible to come alive and speak so much more passionately or emphatically than anything that I could drum up on my own.

This group also tends to be the group that decides what book of the Bible we'll go through next. I remember when we were wrapping up the Book of Daniel and considering a three- or four-week tour through a New Testament book. We hadn't settled on which one, so I suggested Titus to the Sermon Discussion Group. We spent most of one discussion time reading and talking through the first two chapters of Titus. By the end of the night, the group was leaning away from Titus and I was "commissioned" to consider going in another direction. By the end of the week, I decided to pursue the book of 1 Corinthians instead.

This conclusion wasn't made because we didn't like the Book of Titus, but because we felt the best way to interact with the complicated story of church leadership that consumes much of that letter did not fit our situation for a Sunday night gathering. A few days after that group, I received an e-mail from Wes, a forty-nine-year-old computer analyst who was a regular at the Sermon Discussion Group. Wes not only contributed during the discussion on Tuesday nights but also continued thinking and adding to the dialogue on his own and occasionally let me in on this process.

Hi Doug,

I think we had an enjoyable and interesting discussion which, as you commented, has a fairly limited application. Questions like, "Is this statement too culturally bound to be useful?" or "Do we know enough about the context to provide a balanced commentary?"—these are important questions, but I'm afraid they became a little debilitating for us. I feel we found ourselves unable to identify the core issues the text itself is addressing and to allow it to ask its questions of us. Generally, I think Titus is asking us, do we have what it takes to flourish as a group? What sort of understandings, hopes and dreams are driving the enterprise? What kinds of people need to be at the tiller? What kind of people should we be generally in order for the group to flourish? What kinds of things need to be talked about so we can grow? Are we able to respond to adversaries with wisdom and steadfastness? Do we have adversaries (if not, why not?), and what do they look like? I think we could almost have another Sermon Discussion Group about this, a little more creative about the themes and meanings and less analytical. But I'm still not sure we need to actually do Titus right now. Maybe the issues aren't compelling for us. I'll be supportive of any decision. I hope this helps.

Wes

For me, this is what makes the Sermon Discussion Group different from a Bible study.

WE AREN'T JUST GETTING TOGETHER TO READ AND EXTRACT FROM THE BIBLE.

Rather, this group is like a microcosm of our community. In many ways, this group sets the form and feel and content for what will happen on Sunday night during our gathering. Together, we explore the questions and issues on a small scale so that when the same passage is presented to the larger group, it will be clear that it has been wrestled with, not just by theologians, but by "regular" people as well.

The people at the Sermon Discussion Group know they aren't just there to deepen their own understanding of the Bible but to stand in for others as we enter into the passage on behalf of the greater community.

Each week, we end the group with someone offering a paraphrase of John 14:25-26, where Jesus says, "All this I have spoken while still with you. But the Advocate, the Holy Spirit, whom the Father will send in my name, will teach you all things and will remind you of everything I have said to you." We trust the Holy Spirit as the arbiter and teacher of truth during our time together, so with this prayer we ask the Spirit to keep in our minds that which we said that was in agreement with the ways and teachings of Jesus.

WHY WE TALK ABOUT THE BIBLE

The Bible Discussion Group serves as my primary time of preparation for the sermon, not only because it gives me a better idea of how to focus what I'm going to say, but because I like the idea of the sermon being created out of something more than just my thoughts and research on a passage.

Whenever people are digging into an issue, they hear various opinions and ideas. In our information-frenzied world, we have all developed very effective ways of deciphering whom we listen to and whom we do not. If this were not the case, we would simply believe every billboard, TV commercial, and telemarketing call we receive. We are used to judging new thoughts and allowing or disallowing them to have authority in our lives.

So there is no need for us to stop every unwanted comment. The protection from wrong belief comes from having an integrated and involved community of people who engage in one another's lives, not from limiting what is presented. The censoring approach does not serve anyone—not the originator of the idea who may need to hear herself say it to know if she believes it, nor the hearer who may need to hear it before he determines that he doesn't hold to it.

We all hold beliefs that are heretical or goofy to one degree or another. The value of being in a community where we discuss our beliefs and thoughts is that our understanding of the things of faith is allowed to sit in the company of so many other people's ideas and beliefs, which allows us to see our own more clearly. We are not left to ourselves to obtain right belief, nor are we given the impression that only a select few members of the body can be trusted to instruct us in the ways of faith.

Wes recently commented on his upbringing in a faithful Christian home. According to him, the Bible was seen as the ideal partner of the well-educated mind in creating perfect knowledge. Wes went on to say that in his family, the goal of spiritual formation was that a person would know precisely what should be known. Those who disagreed with the "correct" position were seen as the opposition that needed to be attacked. There was little room for dialogue. Part of Wes' self-disclosed enjoyment of the Sermon Discussion Group is that it has greatly dispelled the cut-and-dried attitude of his upbringing. He contends that the approach of Solomon's Porch has modeled working through struggle—not just the struggle with ideas, but with turning those ideas into a thoughtful, intentional life in the way of Jesus.

For those who find little struggle in life and faith, dialogue might seem like an unproductive, tangent-ridden waste of time. For those for whom struggle is a constant companion, dialogue is a crucial practice of faith. It is my suspicion that there is something more to the practice of dialogue than its benefit to the participants.

The Inventive Age has brought with it a need for us to learn to listen to those with whom we disagree—it has become impossible to shut them out or separate ourselves from them. This isn't simply a move toward being more tolerant people, but toward being salt and light in the world. We simply cannot bless the lives of others without a willingness to engage in conversation with them.

At its worst, the Inventive Age, with its endless access to ideas and information, can leave people wanting to pull inward and congregate only with like-minded others. We see it in politics, in religion, in governments. All the diversity of ideas becomes so overwhelming that we want to retreat to those places where certainty and sameness reign.

But at its best, the Inventive Age allows us to discover ways of thinking we never knew existed. It allows us to break out of our tendencies toward hyper-individualism and find places of connection with people who might be very different from us. And that's kingdom living.

WE ARE ALL CALLED TO LEARN FROM AND LISTEN TO THOSE WHO WOULD CHALLENGE US AND NOT JUST THOSE WHO AGREE WITH US.

It's important to note that a dialogue is not a debate. For dialogue to be effective, we need to resist the urge to cut people off and fix what they say. The purpose of entering into dialogue is not only to come to our own conclusions but to enter into the reality of the other. Our hope at Solomon's Porch is that our practice of healthy dialogue will not end as we leave our meetings or gatherings but will form new habits in us and make us into new people.

Forming new ways is often difficult. There are times when the discussion following the sermon does not go down the path I had hoped, and, in my opinion, becomes less than useful. There have been times when people share observations that are not particularly helpful. There have even been occasions when people have used the discussion to "take us to task" for issues that are at times legitimate and other times not so much. I can tell you that it can be very difficult to sit there and listen to people offer critiques that seem less-than-valid. That's not just true for me as a pastor, but for us as a community.

This is what makes the pursuit of spiritual formation through dialogue so hard. We are forced to listen as well as talk. We are forced to consider ideas that are not our own, and might never be. We are forced to live openly and graciously within a community of people we might not always agree with. Let me assure you, this is much harder work than delivering a well-crafted message. In dialogue you are not allowed to stay right where you are; you must move toward the perspective of the other person. You don't need to stay there, but a commitment to community means that you are required to visit.

It's also become clear to me that dialogue works best when it's face to face. The Inventive Age might take its name from the endless advances in technology, but oddly enough it has led to people valuing face-to-face contact in a way they haven't before.

The people in our community are very comfortable with technology, and most are young enough that they don't remember much about life without computers and the Internet. So when we set up our Web site, I expected our online bulletin board and chat rooms to fill up quickly. They didn't. Our Web site has recently gone through an update, but people still don't use it much. We have to remind people to look for us on Facebook. I've been surprised that, outside of specifically orchestrated efforts, our efforts to be a proprietary online church have been a complete failure.

It's not that we aren't Internet people—our folks seem to use Facebook and Twitter to connect with each other almost constantly. But we don't use our church site as a primary means of connection.

I don't know if this is something specific to our community or if there is something about person-to-person conversation that leaves the cyber-community approach wanting. My hunch is that when given a choice between a personal conversation and a virtual one, most people would rather see the tears, hear the laughter, hold the hand. People like to be heard, they like to have a voice, they want to make an impact and be impacted by others. Dialogue allows those things to happen.

REACH OUT

A planter plants her every dream in the ground
And goes to bed each day and prays
For rain to come, come drenching down all-around
But only wakes to skies of blue.

For so long now she reaches down deep for evidence.
Persistence she thought should now
Give God a reason enough to rain down
But everything is dry around

"You should let it go there's always tomorrow.
Give it time," they always say.
"What will be will be. Don't force it."
"It's better this way."

But, have you ever been so near to something
That to see it you have to reach out,
Reach out as if blind?

Reaching out past every circumstance isn't everything.
Maybe live within the gray.
I've tried before to hold my every glance as only chance.
It brings me back to why I pray.

Have you ever been so near to something
That to see it you have to reach out,
Reach out as if blind?

—Ben Johnson

CHAPTER 8
ABUNDANCE

When I was a kid and didn't want to finish the food on my plate, my mom would say "There are children starving in China" (to which I wanted to say, "Well how about I pack it up and send it to them?"). The idea was that there was not enough food in the world and a righteous act was to honor the scarcity of the food by eating what was available to me. Today there is more than enough food in the world. The problem is the distribution of those resources to the people who need it.

The Inventive Age requires that we recognize that we live a world where what we need is available. The charge of the church is to connect the need with the abundance.

In the entrance to the natural food co-op where we shop, there's a quote from Wendell Berry painted on the wall. It says, "What we need is here." This is not just a statement of the great food selection, it is an Inventive Age view of reality.

Deeply embedded in the ethos of our community is the assumption that everything we need is in our midst. This belief is informed by a trust that God is more engaged in our world than we are and the people who join us in our community bring with them gifts, perspectives, and qualities that are sufficient. When we pursue the practice of hospitality and share our lives with others, we are doing more than giving and receiving gifts. We are being reminded that we live in a world of abundance.

To tweak a phrase from William Gibson, the future is already here, it's just not evenly distributed. We do what we can to engage in one another's lives in order to bring out what we already have at our disposal.

This might be something Jesus was getting at when he responded to the question of when the kingdom of God would come. He said, "The coming of the kingdom of God is not something that can be observed, nor will people say, 'Here it is,' or 'There it is,' because the kingdom of God is in your midst" (Luke 17:20-21).

WEDNESDAY NIGHT DINNERS

It's the Wednesday after Easter and we are hosting the weekly community dinner at our house. For me, the Wednesday night meal is one of the highlights of my week. These meals involve nearly every element of our life as a community. This is when I often see us blessing each other's lives in tangible, meaningful ways.

Even though the meal doesn't start until 6:30, people begin arriving around 5. We're not quite ready for people to be here, but we're glad to have the help; there will be something like fifty people arriving for dinner.

Our family hosts the weekly meal about once a month and we've learned that these meals require a certain level of coordination. We announce the location on Sunday nights and invite the entire community to eat together, so we never know how many people will show up; it could be ten, it could be sixty.

The Solomon's Porch folks tend to be last-minute kind of people, so our phone has been ringing all Wednesday afternoon with people calling to ask what they can bring. People really like to contribute to the meal. This is more than the strong Midwestern sense of needing to help. People like to feel they are part of the meal, like they aren't just showing up but actually joining in as co-hosts for the night. It really does feel more like a family gathering than a church supper. There is no agenda, no meeting, no ulterior motive but to be together and share our lives over a meal. It's not about getting a free meal, but opening our lives to one another over a meal.

Tonight, Shelley is preparing enchiladas: regular and vegan versions. We have several vegetarians and others with special diets in our community, so it's a fairly common practice to provide a few different meal options for the Wednesday night dinners and other community meals. Making more than one entree is not just an act of Minnesota nice, it is a true gift of hospitality that sends the message that everyone is welcome; everyone belongs.

By 6, the house is filling with conversation and the activities of setting-up and meal preparation. We intentionally save a few jobs—setting the tables, tossing the salad, setting out the plates—until people arrive. Not only are these things more easily done with additional help, but it's another way of letting people know they are part of the "family" and they have something to contribute.

The result is a house hopping with people. Many are just standing in the way in the kitchen, where people tend to congregate, but others are going through our cupboards to find glasses, moving tables around in the dining room, and cutting vegetables at the kitchen table. The family room is crawling with young children, and the older kids are outside playing on the trampoline—there will be seventeen children on this night.

Children are an integral part of our community and these meals are no exception. On this night, our daughter, Michon, is playing with Mindy's four daughters, and our three sons are jumping on the trampoline with Josiah, Emily, Isaac, and Lydia. This gives the parent of these children the chance to pitch in, serve, and be served by others without having to focus solely on their children.

The house is starting to get warm and it smells wonderful. Our children's anticipation of "who is going to be here tonight?" is growing.

About 6:15, we hit a hitch. Kathryn, who isn't familiar with our oven, didn't realize that she needed to set the oven to bake when she set the temperature, so the enchiladas haven't been cooking. Actually, it's not a big deal. We normally eat at 6:30, but there are always people trickling in late, so tonight we'll eat at 7. Usually, we can rotate the latecomers in to the dining room as others finish their meals. We'll be a little more crowded tonight, but we'll manage.

When the meal is ready, we invite those joining us for the first time to sit at the main table where we put our finest silverware and the good dishes. We do this to honor them as our special guests and to give them the chance to meet the most people. The rest of us cram in around them in our much too small dining room.

Shelley asks a blessing on all who are in our home and we eat. Some kids head to the kitchen, others to the basement. A few people stand in the kitchen to eat as they help set out desserts and fill water pitchers. There are four tables in the dining room/living room seating nearly thirty people. We actually encourage people to squeeze into a place at a table so that we can all be together rather than spread out all over the house. I look at all these people sharing stories, laughing, passing the salad, serving each other, and I know I'm looking at something beautiful; this is an act of mutual hospitality.

As dinner ends, desserts are offered and dishes are gathered. Shelley and I don't feel the need to orchestrate anything; people simply do what they see needs to be done. A few people are cleaning dishes, breaking down the folding tables, moving chairs and table leaves, and putting things back where they belong.

Others settle on the couch to talk or gather in the kitchen to pick over the crumbs of dessert. Everywhere, there are conversations. As hard as it is to drag their kids away, parents are starting to gather their young children. Others collect stray shoes for them and buckle babies into car seats. It's clear that this meal is not just something we are hosting, but that people are hosting each other in our house.

By 10:30 the house is free of guests and Shelley and I head to bed.

Lying there, I reflect on what a difference it is to pastor people who eat, serve, and clean in my home, people whose homes I will eat, serve, and clean in on another Wednesday night. What a difference it is to open not only our church and faith to others, but our home, refrigerator, cupboards, and closets to them.

I don't feel like I am somehow in authority over these people, or that I need to keep some kind of professional boundary with them. It feels really good. This is the kind of life I had dreamed of.

Then the worry kicks in. As is typical of my obsessive personality, I begin thinking about the people who weren't here and normally would be and wonder if anything's wrong. I replay the interactions of the night and think of those who didn't seem to engage with anyone. I think about those who might feel lonely and isolated even in the midst of this night. It's sometimes frustrating to me that I can't force people to feel as connected as I do in our community.

Then I start thinking about next week's dinner at Ben and Jen's and find myself hoping that next week everyone will take that "magical step forward" into the kind of life I envision us living. Finally, I concede that it won't. I decide to quit thinking about it and fall asleep still glad there is a next week when we will gathering together and serve one another again.

THE COMMON TABLE

We eat a lot of meals together. In addition to the Wednesday meals, there is a men's breakfast every Tuesday morning, with no agenda beyond cramming into a small Cuban restaurant and having breakfast, a women's brunch on Sundays, a huge potluck brunch at someone's home after our Easter sunrise service, and a gathering at a local burrito place each Sunday after church that often feels more like church than many official church services I have been part of.

And we share meals with people outside of our community as well. Every other month, people from Solomon's Porch plan, prepare, and serve a meal to the homeless and working poor through an organization called Loaves and Fishes. Some people volunteer to bring ingredients for the meal, others make the food, others serve it, others clean up. We have recently started working with an organization called Claire Housing that provides housing for people in the last stages of HIV-related illnesses. Several people from the Porch prepare and share meals with the people living in a Claire Housing home just down the street from the church.

In addition to the many planned and impromptu meals people of our community have with one another, we usually have food available at our gatherings and we encourage people to enjoy a cup of tea or a peanut butter sandwich whenever they like. We keep some food in a refrigerator at the church so that anyone working in the building can find something to eat or drink.

People often bring meals to the gatherings—there's a Chinese restaurant across the street from the church that I think we've been keeping in business for the last four years—and eat in the Family Room before church. Others bring food on Sundays to send home with families that needed extra help for one reason or another. Another group of people do a meal exchange where they trade home-cooked food with a few other families so that everyone gets four or five meals to take home with them. Some of these acts of hospitality are formal parts of the church schedule, others are simply ways of caring for each other.

HOSPITALITY IS A SIGN OF ABUNDANCE.

Hospitality says "there is enough for us all and you are welcome." Here in Minnesota, hospitality is often synonymous with food. But we are working to make sure our hospitality is not limited to meals. For us, it's really about involvement in each other's lives and the act of welcoming the stranger; if you were to join us for these meals, you'll find families, singles, people in their fifties, people in their teens, people who are new to our community and people who have been here since the start. These are people who might never have entered into each other's lives but for the fact that they are sharing a meal.

Dinners hosted in homes are not just events of the church but also serve as a place for us to practice our kingdom living. When we join each other in the common rituals of stirring the soup, washing the plate, or folding the tablecloth, we are entering into the most basic places of life. When a person sits in someone's house, on their couch, at their table, they are brought to a place where they tend to be more honest, more open, more vulnerable. They move closer to their true selves, to the place where spiritual formation accelerates.

At the same time, hospitality is not solely about people who get along spending more time together. It is really about welcoming the outsider, the needy, or those from whom we are disconnected. Communal meals force people to eat with those they may not care for—this is the result of living a habitual life of hospitality. We desire to live in reconciled relationship with each other, but that can be very hard to do. Our insecurities, sin, and selfishness get in the way. But regular acts of hospitality demand that we take stock of how we're doing.

When you see someone you don't care for at the mall, you can look the other way or duck into a store. You can avoid those same people at church by turning your attention to the "religious" activity or simply avoiding eye contact. But the intimacy of eating a meal together puts unreconciled relationships in a different context. You can't pass the salad dressing without looking at the other person. You might have to squeeze past them on your way to your chair or hand them your dirty plate. It's hard to maintain the separated individualistic mentality of isolation when you're sharing a meal.

But hospitality isn't just about the host. The beautiful twin of sincerity is invitation and invitation is about the other, about asking them into your life. When you invite someone to come into your home, you are telling that person that you accept her, that you trust her enough to show her new parts of yourself. When people visiting Solomon's Porch for the first time are invited to a Wednesday meal— and they always are—they are being included in one of our most intimate celebrations. They are invited to become part of our community.

When hospitality is seen only as having food together, it is possible for it to no longer be a means of spiritual formation but an end in itself. It's possible for someone to come to a Wednesday night dinner or a Tuesday morning breakfast for no other reason than to eat. It's possible for a person to fill their plate then leave without making any real connection. It's possible for a person to miss out on the real ways lives are blending and changing over Shelley's strawberry salad or Michelle's gluten-free bread. But for those who want their lives to be touched, I believe they find real spiritual growth through efforts of sincere, invitational openness of hospitality.

There is a kind of "patent leather" spiritual formation (a glossy, slick substitute for the real thing) that involves little vulnerability or self-disclosure. It may feel nice to sit in a Sunday-school class and listen to someone talk about spirituality and belief but not have to open yourself up to its implications. There is a certain ironic comfort that comes with a life built around looking the part on the outside while wilting away on the inside.

But when a friend tells you about a deep struggle, and the natural response is to enter in to that person's life, whatever the risk, it is in these times that we find ourselves being transformed into the people of grace and mercy opened for us in Kingdom of God life. Hospitality doesn't mean we ignore personal boundaries, but when it comes to making personal connections with others, many of us have boundaries that are too high, that prevent us from moving past the veneer of "everything's fine."

At its core, hospitality is an act of faith. It is faith in God and faith in people. It is an open posture that views others not as a threat, but as participants in the process of one another's redemption. When we recognize that each of us is part of the whole and that in the whole we find what we need, then the abundance of our world appears.

I'm reminded of a song by Bruce Springsteen where he describes a man who has a tattoo on each hand, one that reads "Love" and one "Fear." In the song, Springsteen suggests that it was never clear which hand held his future. This is the choice we all face—will we reach out with love and possibility or fear of limitation? Which future will we create? This choosing comes easier for some than others. But there is no doubt in my mind which hand holds the gospel.

A while back, Steve made an announcement on a Sunday night that he needed help for a family he had just met. He told the story of meeting a young man as part of a youth camp he was at during the week. The boy was discussing struggles at home and how he wished his family would keep the house clean. When camp was over, Steve took this boy home and discovered that the house was not just messy, but had been condemned by the health department earlier in the week. The boy and his siblings would end up in the care of the state if the parents didn't get the house in livable condition.

That night our community was invited to help clean the house so the boy's family could move back in. Every day for the next week, there were people from our community in that house filling dumpster after dumpster of decades-old items, rotten food, dead animals, and rancid carpet. Much work is needed with this family not only in getting and keeping the house clean but in dealing with the psychological issues that created the situation in the first place.

It turned out the family was involved with a church that was not previously aware of their situation. We made arrangements with their church that we would clean the house so they could spend time getting the family the help they needed in other areas. People from Solomon's Porch went to that house and cleaned the garbage of strangers, with a stench so bad they had to cover their faces, not for pay or out of professional obligation, but because they knew that loving and caring for those in need is part of their becoming like Jesus. It was a Holy week.

MAINTAIN

As we face forward facing familiar
Remember our posture will help form belief
And remember to turn, kneel, and reach out a hand.
To be sure and look past what's captive in "me."

As we look onward imagine a dancer
A member of life created to be
One movement, a spin, turn, we live it firsthand
Like a liquid life lesson you've got to swim it to see.

Freedom is not given only
To those of us who need release from a cell or disease
Maybe it should be a space we maintain
And we have a blessing to be.
And we have a blessing to be.

Now we are stewards a part of creation
Knowing great valleys and rivers we keep
Humbly we touch, give and cradle the land
Maintaining a gift God invites us to be.

Freedom is not given only
To those of us who need release from a cell or disease
Maybe it should be a space we maintain
And we have a blessing to be.
And we have a blessing to be.
And even the price of this notion
That Christ has displayed in devotion
Propels and compels us to be
Not just well but a part of the motion

Freedom is not given only
To those of us who need release from a cell or disease
Maybe it should be a space we maintain
And we have a blessing to be.
And we have a blessing to be.

—Ben Johnson

CHAPTER 9
OPEN-SOURCE BELIEF

The success of the Information Age produced a strange outcome—a lack of trust in knowledge. With so much information, some of it was bound to conflict. And it did, leading to a loss of confidence in the idea of certainty. Belief has become a temporary state. Take the egg for instance. In my adult life the egg has been both maligned and celebrated. It has gone from being "incredible and edible" to being a heart clogger. Then the whites that were okay. Then the yolk was back in favor. Then only eggs from free-range chickens were acceptable. Or consider the now-famed tobacco executives who testified before Congress that there was absolutely no way their product could cause health concerns. Or the politician who was certain of the accuracy of the intelligence before voting for an act of war only to later admit to the limitations of what they knew. Or the financial advisor who recommended mortgage-backed securities. Or the scientists who assured us of the shuttle's safety.

Inventive Age sensibilities allow us to see belief as a process and not a settled fact, as experiences, not conclusions. When we declare our belief we are really giving a snapshot of our current best understanding—this is where I am now and might be later. Or maybe not.

Now I think belief has always been this way, but it's taken the Inventive Age to unwrap it from the veil of certainty for good. In fact, in the Inventive Age the temporary nature of belief is seen as strength. The Information Age was a time when wonder or doubt was a liability and certainty was a strength. Now doubt, change, and wondering are seen as the fabric of a strong belief. To share one's limited knowledge is a must. Blinding confidence is a sign of weakness.

While this cultural notion of conditional belief seems appropriate in business and government, it can be a much harder sell in the area of religion. For many, religion is about faith and not facts—you believe in spite of what you know.

In our community, we have chosen to allow people to express their changing beliefs without fear of repercussions. I'm not sure we have any more people who doubt and wonder than other churches, but I do think we have more people who feel comfortable inviting others into that process with them.

I received this message from Danielle who has been in a state of flux in her beliefs for the entire three years she has been part of our community. As a mother of three children under the age of five, a recovering addict who was raised in a Pentecostal church tradition, and a recent college graduate, she has seen most of her once-core beliefs shaken and dismantled. Not long ago, she wrote to me.

Doug,

Thank you, for your friendship and for
your compassion toward me. I still eagerly await
the day that we can sit and talk God stuff—I have
so much to say, and so many questions—but
until then, there's something I've been meaning
to tell you. Take it for what it is, but in the past
year or more it seems my questions and ponder-
ings on the Bible and spiritual matters in general
keep leading me to one place. It's almost scary to
admit it, like a coming out, but I find I feel most
at peace with agnosticism (even agnostic atheism). So do with that what you will, but I tell you
this because I feel so strongly that being a part
of SP has been healing and beneficial as a part of
this journey. When I was talking to my husband
about this recently, I said, "I just feel like SP has
let me grow into my atheism." I hear that and I
know that might make some people shudder, but
for me it is beautiful. The more I come to terms
with that belief, the less angry I feel. I would wa-
ger a guess that this is just one step on the path,
that I may not end here with this belief, but in the
meantime I am happy with it. For now.

So there you go. Be well, friend.

Danielle

To me the significance of this message is not where
she's at in her belief. It's that she feels she can be part of
our community even while she feels this way.

There is an African adage: "He who travels alone
travels fastest. He who travels together travels furthest." I
think we are called to travel far and not fast in our belief.

DREAMS

In the early days of Solomon's Porch, we met together and shared our dreams for Solomon's Porch. We didn't have a predetermined picture of how we wanted this experiment to unfold; we were seeking something new, together. We didn't look at handbooks or guides to starting a church. We had no interest in doing a "cover" version of someone else's church model. We knew there were aspects of our pasts that were useful, beautiful, and could benefit others, and we knew there were still other aspects of faith we had little or no exposure to.

We often asked a key question of one another:

"WHAT IN YOUR PAST WAS LIFE-GIVING? HOW COULD WE INCORPORATE THAT INTO OUR LIVES TOGETHER?"

The basic elements of our community came from these discussions, and we have sought to continue this invitational creative process over the last eleven years.

We started our community with a list of twenty-six dreams. We often say that we want the dreams of Solomon's Porch to reflect the dreams of the people in our community. We want that list to keep growing and changing with us. It was never meant to be stagnant. Recently,

WE DREAM OF A CHURCH WHERE:

1. We listen to and are obedient to God

2. People who are not Christians become followers of God in the way of Jesus

3. Those who are not involved in church would become an active part of it

4. People are deeply connected to God in all of life; body, mind, soul and spirit

5. Beauty, art and creativity are valued, used, and understood as coming from the Creator

6. Culture is met, embraced and transformed

7. Joy, fun and excitement are part of our lives

8. The kingdom of God is increased in real ways in the world

9. The Biblical story of God is told and contributed to

10. Biblical justice, mercy, grace, love and righteousness lead the way

11. Truth, honesty and health are a way of life

12. We value innovation and are willing to take risks in order to bring glory to God.

13. Worship of God is full, vibrant, real, and pleasing to God

14. Faith, hope and love are the context for all

15. The next generation of leadership is built up and leaders are servants

16. Everyone is equipped to do ministry

17. God's Spirit takes precedence over all structures and systems

18. Christian Community is the attraction to outsiders and the answer to questions of faith

19. People participate in the kingdom of God in accordance with their abilities and gifts

20. We are connected to, dependent on and serve the global Church

21. People learn the ways of God and are encouraged to make it central to their lives

22. Other churches are valued and supported

23. People's visions and ideas of ministry come to life

one of our working groups decided to update that list and is in the process of breathing life back into it. They are working with our artists and musicians to put visual and musical bones on these ideas that have been floating around us for all this time.

This idea of bringing our dreams to a new church start is quite different from the model of the "program" church many of us had experienced. We weren't drawn to the kind of church where the community becomes a collection of services meant to meet the felt needs of the waiting masses. We never wanted Solomon's Porch to be a place where people were "serviced."

A few years before the start of Solomon's Porch, Shelley and I were visiting a church that met in a school cafeteria. There was a couple sitting in front of us, and while we never actually met them, we did feel a strange connection with them after staring at the backs of their heads for an hour. As the service ended, the husband turned to his wife and, in the midst of a yawning stretch, said, "Well, that wasn't so bad."

That's the kind of thing I say when I get up from the chiropractor's table or when I get my oil changed in less than thirty minutes. At that moment, I knew that if Solomon's Porch—just an idea at the time—ever happened, I didn't want it to become a provider of religious goods and services, no matter how hip or polished they were.

I believed the church could be more, that it was reasonable to hope for a deeper response than "That wasn't so bad." From the beginning of Solomon's Porch, we have referred to our time together on Sundays as gatherings and not services. It's a little thing, but it reminds us that we are there to live life together, not simply have our individual needs serviced.

In many ways, learning to walk in the way of Jesus is much like the process of learning our native language; we pick it up when we are immersed in it. I would guess that nearly all of us spoke and communicated long before we started our formal education. What we then learned in school was not the beginning of language use, but the refining of it. In educational settings, the theory of language acquisition through immersion is by far the most successful means of learning.

So it is with Christian faith. Rather than seeing Christianity as belief we acquire in a completed form, we ought to enter into it with the understanding that we are at the beginning of a life-long process of discovery and change. Ours is a faith that is lived, from beginning to end.

How people come to believe things is very complicated business and no one is quite sure how it happens. The question that has gripped us as a community is not if someone should believe or even what they ought to believe. We are more interested in the question of how people come to a place of belief.

We all have some beliefs of which we are quite certain—that the sun will come up in the east tomorrow, that vinegar will taste sour, that it's best to avoid poison ivy. We know why we believe these things and can often even point to a process through which we came to believe them. We think of these beliefs, this "knowledge," as somehow the most authoritative kind of belief, the kind we'd use to build a case about wearing long pants on a hike.

Most beliefs, however, are based on the ways we experience life, on the things that happen to us. We hold our most important beliefs at such a core level we can hardly imagine not believing those things or explaining how we came to such beliefs.

The Information Age operated under the idea that people start out as empty vessels that need to be filled with information in order to obtain knowledge. This idea has produced an educational model of passing on information, a model that is used not only in schools but in business, art, and entertainment. This view is organized around the idea that knowledge is power, that if we give people the information needed to accomplish something, they will do it. The church has co-opted this model and used it as a basis for spiritual formation with such veracity that it is hard for many to imagine a church forming belief through any other means.

The idea that we gain knowledge through information leads to a way of processing information known as foundationalism, a way of thinking about learning as a construction project. The information we acquire is the foundation upon which our hopes, ideas, and experiences rest. The foundation, then, is critical to sustaining belief. When new information that supports the belief is taken in, it strengthens the belief. When information that seems contrary is allowed to penetrate, the foundation is weakened. The belief structure can only tolerate a certain amount of weakening or the entire system might collapse.

The rules of formal debate are based upon this notion: If you can show that someone's belief is built on a faulty premise, then the belief itself can be shown to be faulty and in need of replacement. This is what produced the Inventive Age notion of functional but conditional belief.

I understand the benefits of this way of thinking because I used to operate under this assumption, too. I thought people believed things because they built those beliefs upon certain sets of information, and if I wanted them to believe differently, I simply needed to give them new information. I was good at making my point, deconstructing someone else's point, then helping them replace it with new information that would lead them to the same conclusions I'd made.

Frankly, it would be nice if belief really were that simple. My job would be so much easier if I could send out an e-mail to my church that explained all the stuff of faith and then went to Bermuda for the rest of the year while all that good information soaked into their minds.

BUT IN THE INVENTIVE AGE, IT'S BECOME CLEAR THAT INFORMATION IS RARELY SUFFICIENT TO CREATE BELIEF: IT NEEDS A PARTNER.

The idea that knowledge is power might work well for getting a job or wiring a house but is not enough to build the kind of belief of spiritual formation. Belief is not simply holding to particular understandings; belief is centered in the way we understand and live in the world.

At Solomon's Porch, we are developing practices built on the understanding that belief is formed when information finds a partner with other aspects of our lives— specifically hopes, experiences, ideas, and thoughts. We are not disparaging the cognitive process or suggesting that it's not important that we think right. The question is how we end up thinking right. Look, I have no interest in

going down the tired road of arguing if thinking is more
or less important than feeling. Rather than saying one
is more important than the other, I'm suggesting that in
belief there is always a complicated interaction, like a well-
executed, spontaneous, freeform tango between information and one of the belief partners.

I don't see this as a radically new idea but rather
one that makes sense with the way most people come
to understand new ideas. In Inventive Age settings when
information is suggested to us, we send it through a
complicated grid of criteria. Does what is being suggested
match with what I already know to be reliable? Does what
is suggested fit with my experiences in the world? Does
what is being suggested connect with the way I would like
things to be? Does it fit with what I believe to be possible?
Information waits in the mind like a rider waiting at a
bus stop until it can catch a ride with hopes, experiences,
thoughts, or ideas to the place of belief.

There are people who are quite certain of their
belief that human beings have never landed on the moon.
They contend that what's been seen on television over the
last thirty-five years is a fabrication perpetrated by the U.S.
government in order to deceive us. This strongly held and,
in their opinion, supported belief is not about the facts; it's
about the violation of what they believe to be possible in
this world.

INTEGRATED BELIEF

For me, recognizing that belief is not dependent on
information alone has changed the way I see the process
of integrating belief in my spiritual formation and in the
lives of others as well. A few years ago I had a conversation with a girl who held beliefs about animal rights and
abortion different from my own. As we talked, it became
clear to me that my attempts to share information meant

to counter her information were not at all useful. Her belief was not based on information but on her hopes and experiences.

I began to realize that someone can take in new information, understand it perfectly well, and still not change their belief. Until I said something that gelled with her hopes and experiences, I was going to have no part in her formation of belief.

I discovered there was no need for me to attempt to deconstruct her foundational belief—she wasn't going to let me and I really didn't feel a desire to. Rather, it seemed right to enter her life as an invited guest, one she could trust to suggest she swap her hopes. After that conversation, I began to wonder what my role as a spiritual guide would look like if it was predicated not on me providing religious information, but on serving as an interpreter and suggestor of alternative dreams, desires, and possibilities. The more I considered this option, the more excited I became.

It's hard to get around the idea of belief as a relational process. People who can change our beliefs are people to whom we give authority to suggest alternatives to us. At Solomon's Porch, our desire is to form friendships where we are invited into each other's lives with a level of trust that allows for spiritual formation. We can learn from one another because we have proven ourselves trustworthy.

There are people who get concerned when they think about knowledge this way. It feels relativistic, as though all ideas are open for reconsideration and the whims of those who are offered those ideas. But the truth is, that's really how belief works. We all hold beliefs that work quite well in our current settings, but fail miserably when we try to transport them to other situations.

This is often the case with students who enter college, or adults who move to other countries. We still know the same things, but our beliefs change because of our new situations. That process is disconcerting for many people, but it happens to most of us at some point or another. Sometimes it happens in the face of tragedy, where all that we thought we knew is thrown down and replaced by an experience that isn't very nice. All that we learn after that point of reorientation will partner with the experience of the tragedy.

There is a kind of challenge in living a faith based on more than information, on allowing it to be connected to the frailty of our humanity. There is something good in the malleability of how we come to believe. In our community, we've found that this understanding of belief actually helps us take risks by keeping us open to the ideas we haven't had yet.

It's been my experience that crisis comes when we are forced to question something we're not ready to question. When we accept that everything is questionable at one point or another, we are more inclined to talk through those questions we were not planning to address. It's a beautiful thing when in the course of our Sermon Discussion Group someone expresses an idea to which someone else says, "I've never thought of it that way!" The sense that spiritual formation is happening in that moment is palpable.

In our community, we've found that mingling information with hopes, experiences, ideas, and thoughts often brings with it wonderful surprises. The process of bringing information alongside belief partners creates a fascinating kind of circularity where all of the partners shift and grow with the contributions of the others. My belief that God is loving will be affected when the hopes of an infertile couple are fulfilled in a pregnancy. That experience will affect the way I talk about God's love with someone else.

Their experiences will affect the way they respond to my words, and their response will affect the way I talk about God's love in the future. This process in no way devalues information, but elevates the partners of belief to that same appropriate level of importance.

LIFE DEVELOPMENT FORUMS

In 2002, we began offering our version of adult formation "classes." Our Life Development Forums are meant to give us the opportunity to lead one another in many areas of life. They are not limited to things religious, but are designed to give us a place to help one another live life in the way of the kingdom of God.

The things of the kingdom life are the ordinary, everyday issues of earthly life. So our forums have covered topics such as learning Spanish, studying the Old Testament, doing massage, learning to discover our areas of strength, poetry, dating, photography, natural health, parenting, and budgeting. These forums are chances for people to share information, hopes, desires, ideas, and experiences of how we can arrange our lives in good, healthy, productive ways.

PROFESSIONS OF FAITH

Our attempts to partner information with our dreams and experiences have led us to create and incorporate written and spoken statements of belief into our community life. We've found this to be a powerful way for people not only to learn but also to participate in a confession of belief. Sometimes we use a well-known piece like the Apostles' Creed or a particular section from the Bible, like the Doxology from Jude that we say after communion. Other times we use prayers from the rich history of Christianity.

I have to admit, this is new territory for me. I used to think that to ask someone to profess something they didn't yet believe was tantamount to making them lie. I couldn't understand why we would ask someone to say something in a crowd they were not comfortable saying on their own.

But I've come to see that the process of believing anything begins with an act of trying it on.

For some, we cannot fully believe something until we've said it out loud to see how it feels and sounds. (For some, this speaking is internal and for others external.) It is as if believing follows the confession. When we invite people to confess a faith that is not yet fully theirs, we are asking them to walk into faith and spend time there.

BIBLE AS AUTHORITATIVE COMMUNITY MEMBER

Through the centuries, there have been various visual and verbal metaphors used to describe the church's relationship with the Bible. Some traditions carry the Bible into worship over their heads showing their submission to it. Some speak of the Bible as the foundation on which they stand. Some view it as a clue book to the faith of the past.

At Solomon's Porch, we find all of these postures helpful. In addition, we speak of the Bible as a member of our community of faith—a very important member that must be listened to on all matters on which it speaks. When we read the Bible in our community, we attempt to fully engage ourselves in it and the God who inspired its creation. We work to listen to the community of faith that has produced us, and the God who dwells in us. We focus our efforts on trying to figure out if our lives could be relevant to the story of God, not if the Bible can be relevant to our lives. We can only do this when we allow the information gleaned from the stories of the Bible to couple with our experiences, hopes, and ideas.

There are times when we interact with the content of the Bible and have a really difficult time understanding it. Sometimes it's because of the extreme cultural differences or the way the section was spoken, recorded, or written. Sometimes what we read just seems to violate our sensibilities. One of our more powerful sermon times in the last year was when Tony Jones led us in a discussion of the story of the Sacrifice of Isaac. The text compelled us to consider the ramifications of this story, and none of us liked our options. It is a terrible story, one with no easy resolution. As a community, we wrestled with it, yelled at it, confessed our deep discomfort with it. We didn't leave that discussion with a tidy understanding of the passage. Instead, we were forced to evaluate the usefulness and trustworthiness of the Bible.

In our community, this seems to happen on a regular basis. Perhaps it's that we are an inquisitive group of people, or maybe it's because we look at such large sections of text at a time and are therefore exposed to some of the truly puzzling parts of the Bible. Whatever the reason, we seem to run into "I'm not sure I like what this says" moments fairly often.

Yet we try to treat the Bible like a best friend to whom we have to give the benefit of the doubt. At some point you have to shrug your shoulders and say, "I don't know what she was thinking, but I'm sure she meant well." Just because there are parts of the Bible that seem unpalatable or incomprehensible in our time doesn't mean we should step away from it or ignore it.

Nor are we satisfied with relegating the complex stories of our faith to simple teaching principles. Rather, because the Bible is part of our community, we are called to step toward it and see what it has to offer us in areas of hopes, experiences, thoughts, ideas, and information. We need to allow it to share with us those things that correct us, teach us, and lead us, even when we don't understand it or like them.

Seeing the Bible as a crucial part of our community is a relational commitment that extends beyond any intellectual commitments we will form. The truth of the matter is that much of our trust in the Bible does not come from information that "proves" the Bible to be credible.

WE BELIEVE THE BIBLE BECAUSE OF OUR HOPES, IDEAS, EXPERIENCES, AND BECAUSE OUR COMMUNITY OF FAITH ALLOWS AND REQUIRES US TO BELIEVE.

There's a sense of discomfort in moving toward an understanding of belief that leads us beyond the tradition of education-based learning of the Information Age. In matters of faith, there is no easy way to describe how each of us comes to believe what we believe. We are complex people with tangled histories and it's naïve to think we can somehow come up with a comprehensive system of learning that leads all of us to the same conclusions. We want to live out the conviction that ideas, hopes, experiences, and understandings play essential roles in the life of our community as we continuing to spur each other on to be spiritually formed by our beliefs.

UPWARD AND LOOKING DOWN

Upward and looking down
Bearded wears a crown
A nice romantic way for us to think on it
I suppose kings and thrones they used to fit

Imagine God around
Filling every sound
Down and in-between the need of everything
Instead of up and out above us glaring

Oh, but how an image takes a hold of you.
Oh, we're stuck in place; we made a mold of you.

Larger than the sky
Closer than the cry
Of falling breeze on reeds, they're whispering.
Just as loud as clouds while thundering

Great and nearer
Imbedded healer
Almighty light
The Hope in the plight of the strain

Gracious redeemer
You fed this dreamer
We join in your might
Implied as the spirit proclaims

Almighty light
The Hope in the plight of the strain

—Ben Johnson

CHAPTER 10
CREATIVITY AND BEAUTY

As I wrote in *Church in the Inventive Age*, culture is made of four components: Thoughts, Values, Aesthetics, and Tools. Among the most powerful and often overlooked cultural component is Aesthetics; that which looks, sounds, smells, and feels right is incredibly powerful. Beauty is an Inventive Age requirement.

Think about architecture. The Industrial Age was not concerned with beauty but with function. Factory buildings we purely utilitarian—windowless brick buildings, urban structures that dominated the landscape. The Information Age concerned itself with efficiency and simplicity—corporate offices full of cubicles that could be manipulated for any kind of work or number of people. But in the Inventive Age, beauty and creativity are as important as function and efficiency.

The mission statement of the United States' largest interior design organization, the American Society of Interior Designers, says volumes about the Inventive Age sensibilities. "ASID is a community of people driven by a common love for design and committed to the belief that interior design, as a service to people, is a powerful, multifaceted profession that can positively change people's lives" (ASID.org). Creating a place of beauty is only

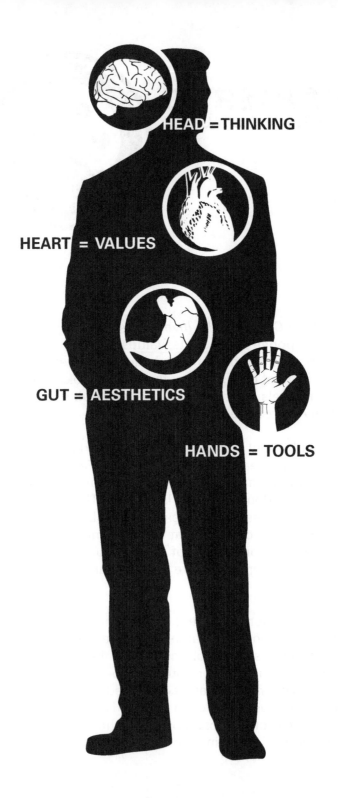

accomplished in community with complexity and love. In the Inventive Age, our environment shapes our cultural expectations.

We have held countless art events in our community over the past eleven years, but there is one that stands out for me as a quintessential Porch event. It was a Good Friday event coordinated by the artists and musicians in our community and it was magical.

Thom Olson, a teacher and artist in our community, helped coordinate the event so I've asked him to tell you more about it. Here's Thom:

It was 7:56 on Friday night and despite our efforts to appear organized and competent, we were still running a half-hour behind schedule. The performances for "The Way Of The Cross" (our version of the fourteen Stations of the Cross commemorating Holy Week) were supposed to begin as soon as people finished walking through our makeshift visual art gallery, which, in this case, consisted of paintings mounted inside the window sills in the row of offices alongside the back wall of our warehouse gathering space.

We thought we'd be done and the performances well underway by then, but a certain pastor (who will remain anonymous but answers to "Hey, Doug") told us to plan for around "seventy-five people or so." A quick head-count confirmed more than two hundred people still waiting in the lobby to come upstairs due to our outmoded (albeit quaint) insistence of ushering people up to the gallery in groups of seven or eight. It was time to formulate Plan B.

I should explain a couple things. First, together with Javier Sampedro and Luke Hillestad, I was involved in coordinating (i.e., herding) the efforts of over thirty painters, sculptors, musicians, actors, and dancers from our community into something that would hopefully resemble a cohesive evening.

Second, each "station" presented that night contained both a visual and performance element; the piece was first depicted visually through a composition mounted on the wall—much like a museum—with the idea that people would file past the pieces in order, then sit down to watch as the same stations were expressed through music, drama, dance, and film. In this way, each person was given more than one opportunity to enter into the retelling of the story. Or at least they'd be able to if we ever got the performances started.

I talked with Luke and Jav and we decided to give it a couple more minutes. "Minnesota nice" strongly influences behavior around here and we agreed that to start with so many people still in the lobby would be rude. We reminded ourselves that one reason we have couches is so people could at least be comfortable while they sat around and waited for us to get our act together.

In spite of how things looked, that night actually represented the culmination of several months of dreaming, planning, and collaborating. Those of us involved in the event met regularly after the Sunday night gatherings for anywhere from twenty minutes to an hour and a half. Each week we'd ask open-handedly, "Anyone got anything they'd like to share or try out?" Invariably, somebody would test out a sample lyric they were working on or get feedback on a new chord progression. Someone might bring a half-finished painting, or attempt to recite a few paragraphs from a not-quite memorized monologue. (Now that's something you don't see every day: artists willing to be vulnerable and risk looking unsophisticated as they share their half-baked ideas with other artists from a wide-variety of backgrounds.)

Part of what made the process memorable was the generous cross-pollination between the artistic disciplines; painters offered honest feedback on a dramatic monologue, actors reflected on what moved them in a piece of music, and musicians suggested new ways to clarify and enhance a visual composition. The art we created with one another became an honest expression of our communal ethic: what we do together is far better and more important than what anyone of us can do by ourselves.

Once the night actually arrived, I noticed that some pieces had been totally reworked since our last meeting. And I realized we never really did rehearse the moment where Jesus dies on the cross and the "Christ Candle" gets snuffed out turning the room pitch black. I looked around at the hundreds of candles in this room and it occurred to me that we should probably have thought of that beforehand. Maybe if we blew out several candles after each station's performance we'd make it.

I caught Luke giving me a look. We'd waited long enough and it was time to dim the lights. I guess we'd figure it out as we went along . . .

I have long lived with a real admiration of creative people. I am particularly drawn to people who can imagine what could be and live their lives in such a way as to bring that vision to fruition. Or maybe it's that creative people are a refreshing wind to me because of my almost complete lack of artistic ability. I swear I either have a music learning disability or avant-garde harmonizing capabilities that most people simply have not caught up to yet. Regardless, I am intrigued by those who see the world in ways that others do not.

It's probably not a coincidence that my first involvement with Christianity came in the form of an artistic telling of the story of Jesus. In high school, I attended a passion play with a friend. Knowing nothing of Christianity, I watched this play with growing interest. Even after I realized this was not the kind of "passion" play I was thinking of, I could feel my heart being opened in new ways. I found myself drawn to the story, to the intensity of the experience, to the sheer magnitude of the drama.

By the end, I had a strong sense there was something there that would have my life. It felt natural to follow the instructions of the person on the stage and join others backstage to talk with some "caring people." I walked into a room of strangers hoping to find someone to help me understand this sense I had that there was a pull in this story I couldn't put my finger on.

Once I got backstage, however, the mood changed from one of emotion to one of instruction. As I recall, someone read through a little booklet with the intention of explaining the logic behind what I'd just seen. I listened and learned and decided to give my life to this call. The initial pull toward God came from my soul, but my "conversion" came from my brain. The majority of my mentorship in Christianity from that point on was with people like myself who thought our way through life.

Yet there was still a part of me, a part that admittedly went dormant in the process of my intellectual faith training, that saw artists as mysterious, almost otherworldly. When I was going through my great awakening of seeking after things I knew nothing about, the idea that this process might involve art and story and creativity made sense. I was almost sure there was something of God I needed that I couldn't even see, something that had to come from this place of creation, of vision, not knowledge or intellect. I wondered if a deeper life with God might be found in the hidden corners of the artist's rooms.

As I grew in my knowledge of the faith, there was also staleness growing in me that I knew I couldn't purge on my own. I didn't need someone to "think outside the box;" I could do that. I wanted leaders who could take me to places where thinking was not the center of my spiritual life, but where it could be joined by experience, emotion, and imagination.

When we were conceiving of life at Solomon's Porch, we didn't set out to start a ministry to creative types. I did not presume myself to be one who could reach artists. Rather, I hoped they would reach me, that they would show me those secret places of faith I had only imagined. I hoped I would find God there.

We attempted to find ways for creativity to be sewn into the fabric of our community, not as an add-on, but as a fundamental part of our spiritual formation. The hope was that we would be a community where, as one of our dreams puts it, "Beauty, art, and creativity are valued, used, and understood as coming from the Creator." Again, this was not an attempt to market the church to artists, but an invitation for them to lead our community.

In so many ways, that's what's happened. As Solomon's Porch has grown, we have attracted a number of artists—both professionals and dabblers. Their presence in our community has opened us up to a way of life that allows for spiritual formation through creativity.

Despite my delight at their presence, I had real doubts about how to make artists a vital part of our community, but my concerns were not theological, they were experiential. I had seen churches where art and artists were used to support the agenda of the church, but rarely, if ever, communities where the artists were invited into the level of leadership of the thinkers and preachers.

In the church where I worked for ten years, we had no shortage of people—we had seventeen softball teams for crying out loud. But in our youth ministry and the church as a whole, we often had to hire out for musicians.

There were drama people available, but it seemed as though they were called on mainly to illustrate the spoken sermon, or to break up the routine for a week here and there. There were occasional dinner theater shows and a few pictures hanging on the walls, but artists were almost as hard to find as fill-in nursery workers.

What struck me is not that these people and their attendant gifts weren't there, but that their absence wasn't perceived as a missing piece in our community or of our spiritual formation. Our life and faith was seemingly complete without them. In moving into our life at Solomon's Porch, my concern was that we would fall into that same way of thinking. Without a model for how to make creativity a part of our lives, I wasn't sure we could pull it off.

As it turns out, I underestimated what can happen when creative people are given permission to give life to their dreams. Admittedly, we were in a position of starting with something new, rather than trying to apply new ways of thinking to old models. That allowed us to imbed creativity into our life as a community from the beginning.

It was helpful that we approached the prospect of living as a creative community with a sense of openness mixed with productive cynicism. There can be a tendency in Christian circles, especially when we are venturing into new territory, to complain about how things are. But creativity is providing a new way of living, seeing, hearing, or being, and we were blessed with several people who love the process of seeing a possibility and turning it into something tangible.

We only allowed ourselves to look at something with cynical eyes if were committed to working on it. We weren't going to gripe about contemporary worship music without letting those conversations spur us to create something that moved us away from those concerns and into a new way of understanding. We wouldn't complain about the lack of art in churches without forming a philosophy of the role of art in our community.

Since that time, we have become a community of deeply creative people—not just artists, but people who are full of ideas about how life can be and how we can bring blessings into the world. We have teachers and designers and writers and therapists and yoga instructors and musicians and dancers and actors and all kinds of other people who have committed their lives to exploring new ways of thinking, of expressing, of living. Together, we are working to create a life that we hope is truly beautiful to God.

There's a dilemma that comes up whenever churches think through who they are and who they want to be:

DO WE CREATE PROGRAMS FOR THE PEOPLE WHO ARE HERE OR FOR THE PEOPLE WE WANT TO ATTRACT?

This is particularly true as churches work to live fully in the Inventive Age. We tried to avoid asking that question and instead asked ourselves who we were and what we had to offer one another.

We have never positioned ourselves as a church for artists, but the way we view creativity and the ways in which the passions of the people who are already here work themselves out makes us an attractive home for creative people.

In being faithful to the call of creativity, we've seen Solomon's Porch become a place where imagination, hope, and faith find the room to get to know each other. And what they create together can be breathtaking.

SPIRITUAL FORMATION THROUGH CREATIVITY

Our efforts at living lives of creativity certainly make our community a more beautiful and interesting place to be. Our space is filled with art—paintings, sculpture, photography. About a year ago, a group of our artists, who meet every Monday night to talk and collaborate and share ideas, came up with an ongoing project they called "Porchtraits." Artists who were interested agreed to make portraits of anyone in our community who wanted one. They made an announcement, people signed up to have a porchtrait made, and the artists drew those names out of a hat (or maybe a beret) to see who would create who.

Now, on the big wall that was once the front wall of the church, there are paintings and pencil drawings and photographs of many of the people in our community. There are babies and children, colorful prints and black-and-white photos, oil paintings and computer generated images. These original works of art surround the huge wooden cross that is one of the only remnants of the previous church to live in this building and every week there seems to be a new one added to the collection.

Instead of a Lifetouch picture directory, we have a gallery of images created by and for the people in our community.

Aesthetics—and all that it stirs in us—matters to our community.

CO-RE-CREATORS

This desire to be people who live creatively and for whom creativity is a kind of spiritual formation goes far beyond having lovely drawings on the walls or lots of people with tattoos on our couches. It goes beyond trying to be people who fit in the Inventive Age. Instead, our creativity comes from a desire to live life as people who are created in the image of a creative God, who are invited to be co-re-creators with God.

The Information Age was all about knowledge acquisition. For the church, that meant finding ways to distill the gospel into a message that was easy to pass on from the pulpit, in a pamphlet, during a Sunday-school lesson. During that era, people came to tell and understanding the story of God through a framework of creation, fall, redemption, and exit from this world. This view of God's work in the world essentially tells us that God's relationship with the world sort of cooled off after the fall and didn't really jump back in until Jesus came along.

Aside from the problems created by basically discounting everything between Genesis 3 and the New Testament, my real concern about this idea is that it has a way of marginalizing our human activity in the world. This motif puts humanity in a passive role where we are left with simply having things happen to us—we are created, we are affected by sin, we are redeemed, we are brought to another place. The only thing we do in this scenario is find creative ways to sin. But I am convinced that we are intended for something else.

There is a way of understanding the story that goes more like this: God is the creator of all things and has been re-creating all things through the redeeming work of Jesus the Messiah. God is constantly creating anew.

GOD ALSO INVITES US TO BE RE-CREATED AND TO JOIN THE WORK OF GOD AS CO-RE-CREATORS.

We are not bystanders, nor are we to be inactive. The Gospels are packed with the implication that we have something to give because of our redemption. We are not left with a memory of a God who made the world and is now simply waiting for this world to expire. We are told to go, to make, to build, to speak, to touch, to feed, to create. Those who lived in the time following the death and resurrection of Jesus went out and created something. They formed faith communities that changed the way they lived and ate and used their money. They believed that Jesus was coming back for them soon and yet they lived in such a way as to make their world more like God's kingdom, even if the actual kingdom was on its way.

Our calling is no different. We aid the Spirit in doing the work of the kingdom by making all things better in our time and place.

This understanding of the story implies that creativity is a central activity in the kingdom of God. Imagine what it means to think of the kingdom of God as the creative process of God re-engaging in all that we know and experience. Imagine what it means to wonder if Jesus used so many metaphors for the kingdom of God not because he couldn't find the right words, but because the kingdom is like so many things, and so many things are like the kingdom.

When we participate with God in the re-creation of the world, when we use creativity as a way of making the world better, we behave in ways consistent with the life of God. The practices of creativity build into us the habits and means of being people who are co-re-creators with God, and this is how we are formed.

Our invitation to be involved in the work of God allows—maybe even commands—us to speak life, hope, beauty, and truth into all things.

The gospel invites us into a future life, but not only a future life after this one, a future life during this one. As followers of the way of Jesus we are not destined to leave things the way they are. We are to be a people who bless the world and make it better by creating in it.

In the story of creation, Adam and Eve are called to make new people and to have dominion over all that is. They are not told to just let it run rampant but to make it good and right. Our call to re-creation is to make things the way they ought to be.

Imagine praying the Lord's Prayer through this lens:

OUR GREAT CREATOR,

MAKE THE WORLD DIFFERENT.

MAKE THIS YOUR PLACE.

GIVE TO US IN WAYS THAT WE HAVE NOT

RECEIVED BEFORE.

FORGIVE US—MAKE US NEW.

LEAD US INTO NEW GOOD THINGS AND NOT

INTO TEMPTATION.

This is a prayer of creativity. It is a prayer of the kingdom.

IMAGINATIVE CHRISTIANITY

In the context of Solomon's Porch, art and creativity are not the same thing. Art provides a means of creating a mentality of creativity, but at the same time can be limiting for people who do not understand themselves to be artists. Our ethos is that we need to make room in our personal and collective lives for creative activities.

That might look like attending the opening of an art show in our Family Room gallery space or joining in a song writing forum, but it also might look like leading the preschoolers in a time of dancing and stories or coming up with ideas for helping our Guatemala team raise money for their spring trip. The details are really secondary to the act of living creatively.

Creativity is what allows us to see what can be and step toward it. It is what offers us the hope that the world can be as God would have it.

Over the past few years, I have tried to glean this sense of futurical vision from those in our community for whom creativity is as natural as the beating of the heart. They have shown me that faith without creativity can easily become faith without hope.

Creativity keeps us from being bound by what exists, freeing us to run into the open spaces of what might be. Creativity moves us to participate, giving us permission to join in the work of redemption rather than just watching it happen.

While giving us a sense of the future, creativity also brings a here-and-now vibe to the activity of God. We start feeling like the things of God are happening in our time and place and not only in the memory of our faith. When the songs we sing or the words we read or the images we view are things we created just last week, we are reminded that the context of our faith is this moment and that we have something to bring into this life, right now.

People who join us for a Sunday night gathering at Solomon's Porch will often find bits of the familiar rhythms of a more traditional worship time. But it's been important to us that there be elements of our gathering that reflect the experiences of our community. It is foolishness for those attempting to live in harmony with God to hold on only to the past while there is so much clear God activity happening in the world.

I recognize that extending the activity of God into new areas is scary for some. There was concern when Abram was called into a new land to join in the creation of a new people. There was concern when the nation of Israel was to leave oppression and enter the land that was promised. There was serious apprehension when God's chosen people were told to live without a king.

And yet God met all these fears with creativity. What is the birth of a promised child to a barren woman but an act of creativity? The way the Messiah came into the world was nothing but beautiful re-creation activity.

And so we have moved into our future with the idea that the Kingdom of God is synonymous with the creativity of God. We have sought to find ways to live our lives with imagination, cleverness, inventiveness, and ingenuity.

We have found ourselves trying to figure out the most fitting ways to do particular things in our community. This applies to the arrangement of our facility, the efforts of spiritual formation with children, preaching, and living as good neighbors. We have been in our current building for four years and have spent much of the past year trying to make it more livable. We have painted and redesigned lighting. We planted a vegetable garden and laid paving stones to make the outside space more welcoming. We have taken down walls and built wider doorways. We often say to one another, "Here we go again, making the world better one building at a time." This served as both a means of motivation, but also as a reflection of the belief that we join in the activity of God by making all things better.

FAILURE OF CREATIVITY

Our efforts at creativity almost always have an element of risk to them. Our artists have led us in making this an acceptable way to be. When art, which often comes from the deepest places of a person, is hung on the wall for everyone to see, when a dance is performed with wide-eyed abandon, when a song is sung for the first time, a message is being set that it is permissible to step out, to generate something new, and to risk failing.

Despite all the bragging I have done in this book, there is seemingly no end to the things we have attempted that have not worked. So many, in fact, that I worry that it becomes distracting to people.

From the start, we wanted to re-imagine the physical situation in our gathering space, moving away from a front-facing, stage focused approach to something more in-the-round. For the first two years we used a three-quarters circle, moving to being fully in-the-round in our new, bigger spaces. Ben and I have had endless conversations about the struggles our set-up creates with sound, lighting, and sight lines.

One day, in the midst of struggling with these and other issues that come with having a space that uses normal household furniture, Ben said, "You know, maybe there are really good reason people use stages." It was at this point that we intuitively knew we had a choice to make; we could give in to the tried-and-true convention or put a greater amount of creativity into play.

Now that we have worked out a sufficient number of these issues, we will most likely never go to anything other than meeting in the round. And who knows, maybe in few decades some people in the midst of rearranging their space for the seventh time will say to one another, "You know, there were probably really good reasons people met in the round."

Not all of our efforts at creative living have been so easily solved, however. In an effort to creatively pursue an alternative form of leadership development and community living, the church purchased a six-bedroom house in Minneapolis. The idea was that we'd have several people from our community live in the house, not as roommates, but as participants in an intentional community. After underwriting the cost of the house and struggling to keep in occupied, we sold the house after eighteen months.

This effort failed in part because we didn't have a very well-thought-out plan, but also because failure is sometimes the result when you try something new.

The decision to sell the house wasn't the end of the world, but it was still painful for those of us who had invested time, dreams, and money into the house. While it might be awhile before we decide to become landlords again, we believe the idea behind the house and the vision that led us to try a different kind of community formation is still worth pursuing. And we've had several de facto community houses spring up as our people have rented spare rooms to each other or bought duplexes with the intention of sharing the space with Porch friends.

We've had other creative efforts that didn't turn out the way we imagined. We've worked incredibly hard to create interior spaces that inspire and welcome all who enter, but the building still has a funky smell that we can't kill despite having burned a lot of incense. We've held writing seminars and art exhibits that have been poorly attended. We attempted adding a monthly time of prayer and communion we called a doxology. There was plenty of brilliant, creative thinking behind this attempt, but it never really became an essential part of our life as a community.

But the beauty of creativity as a means of spiritual formation is that even our "failures" breed hope. In most cases when a creative effort doesn't pan out, it's because the execution is flawed, not the dream. What matters isn't that we have the most beautiful flowers or the most atmospheric space or the most well attended events.

What matters is that all of these expressions are authentic outpourings from our community.

There is, for some, an even greater risk involved in becoming co-re-creators in the world. In the eleven years since Solomon's Porch became a reality, I've had more conversations than I can count about the Inventive Age church and why it's seen as a threat to the evangelical way of life. Most often, the concern I hear is that the "postmodern" church has no sense of the Christian tradition, that it wants to scrap everything that's come before it and make something new.

Maybe that's true in some churches that call themselves "postmodern." But from what I've seen, in the Inventive Age church is a desire not to ignore what's come before us but to be informed and inspired by it as we create ways of living in harmony with God in the Inventive Age.

The Inventive Age is not a stand-alone period; it is the culmination of all that the previous ages have produced.

THE GREAT RISK OF THE CHURCH IS NOT IN LOSING OUR TRADITIONS; IT IS LOSING OUR ABILITY TO REIMAGINE.

I really don't know what to do with the approach to faith that tells us all the answers have been discovered and we are simply to apply those answers to our lives. I don't know how we are supposed to worship with songs, prayers, and confessions created for other times and places. And I really don't know how to live out an understanding of the gospel that says I don't have a part to play in what God is doing in the world.

Creativity is at the center of God's image. It is how we see God and talk to God and find our hope in God. I can't figure out any other way to respond to God's re-creation of the world, to God's invitation that we join in as co-re-creators, than to live as creative people.

SHE MOVES

She moves across the waters
And to the farthest place on earth
Looking for the daughters
That will hear her children's prayer

She doesn't have a bias
As she dances through the sky
And sometimes she moves by us
But we mistake her for the wind

And in that place where the water meets the sky
Where dividing lines say their goodbyes

She breathes
She reveals everything that's ever been concealed
She moves
She cures all the wounds that never would have healed
She breathes
She moves and she will not let us go.

She walks among her children
In such an ordinary way
She talks of signs and miracles again
That birth halleluiah

And in that place where the water meets the sky
Where dividing lines say their goodbyes

She breathes
She reveals everything that's ever been concealed
She moves
She cures all the wounds that never would have healed
She breathes
She moves and she will not let us go.

She breathes
She reveals
She moves
And she cures
She breathes
She moves and she will not let us go

—Javier Sampedro

CHAPTER 11
INTEGRATION

The role of service in our community is about us connecting with others. We are seeking to connect our lives with what God and other people are about in our world. We see the acts of our community as bridges to what others are doing.

In this integration, we recognize that we are part of the whole. These activities extend beyond boundaries of country, race, economics, and culture. When we engage with women who are seeking to leave the sex industry in Minneapolis, we are joining in the passion these women have to change their lives. While we may help with needed food, friendship, housing, and counseling, the gift is really not coming from us to her. She extends the gift to us by allowing us to join in her life. We are not just helping; we are integrating.

Integration is removing the barriers that keep people apart. When we serve meals to the "homeless and working poor," we are not simply redistributing, we are entering into their lives. When we build houses in Guatemala, we are not changing their world, we are remaking our world.

The Inventive Age rewards those who find value not only in the pieces but in the whole.

We often send our people off to other places, sometimes for a few weeks, sometimes for a few years, sometimes forever. While we miss them, we send them off with our blessing and our recognition that they will bring us with them, wherever they go.

GUATEMALA

During our first year as a church, we took a group to Guatemala to build homes for people in a small village there. It wasn't a trip designed for "advanced" Christians who needed the next level of discipleship, but one for the many people in our community who were in need of the kind of formation that can only happen in service of others.

At the time, I wondered if we were jumping into this too fast. I thought maybe we should wait until we had more "mature" Christians in our community. But I knew intuitively that we would not get to a place of mature growth without this kind of experience. I had led numerous trips to Central America as a youth pastor and knew that with my connections and those of others we could create an atmosphere that allowed for this formation to take place.

We developed a partnership with a village where our work is not seen as limited works of charity, but where we have developed a long-term partnership with friends we visit year after year. Our Guatemalan family has taught us how to live in the way of Jesus. After fifteen trips and more than fifty homes, sponsoring sixty kids to help them finish high school, and funding the infrastructure to provide Internet access for the poorest in the village, I am more convinced than ever that these kinds of efforts are not the specialized desserts of spiritual formation but are the main course.

Kathryn is one of those original eight people who put Solomon's Porch together. She grew up in church and was one of the kids in my youth group back when I was a youth pastor. She's got a story for you.

Let me set the scene for you. My name is Kathryn Green. I was on staff with Solomon's Porch for the first three years of its life. In January 2003, I escaped my life and moved to Guatemala for a few months. I had been there before. The previous spring I had been a part of Solomon's Porch's annual trip where we build houses in a small village. Every element of that trip appealed to me, and as soon as I returned to the States I began to make plans to return. Eight months after that trip ended, I was back in Guatemala. In the time of which I write, I was in the middle of a three-week study. After Spanish school, I traveled to the city with which Solomon's Porch has a relationship, San Juan La Laguna.

I was studying in a school located in a western city called Quetzaltenango, or Xelá (pronounced Shey-la) for short. The central park square of Xelá was full at all hours with rollaway store carts, students, entertainers, homeless people, and shoeshine boys. Some of the most persistent characters in the square were the shoeshine boys. They were all young, about twelve years old or younger, and always filthy.

I had been warned about the proliferation of shoe shiners, so I felt smug and expert when approached by one or a group. I became deft at rebuffing the shoe shiners, although I never really liked saying no. Solomon's Porch fosters the Christian senses of mercy and justice, and saying no to a poor, dirty child, no matter how annoying or inappropriate his offered service, always felt horrible to me.

When the next boy came around and asked to
shine my shoes, I was wearing running shoes. I explained
to him that they weren't the kind of shoes that get shined,
but I'd like it if he sat down and talked to me. He did, even
though he made it clear that he was in the park to work.
His name was Pedro, and he was nine years old. He lived
a mile or so from the park square and didn't attend school.
He had five brothers and sisters, including a baby brother.
He didn't know his dad. His mom couldn't work because
of all the kids, and Pedro needed to make any money he
could to help his family.

Although I couldn't help Pedro out by letting him
shine my shoes, I did want to give him something. I asked
if he was hungry and he said yes. I asked him if he would
like any McDonald's, and he replied with, "Caja Feliz?!"
which is the Spanish way to say Happy Meal. I said I
would gladly buy him a Happy Meal, and we began to
walk towards the restaurant. Once we got to the perimeter
of the park, which was surrounded by benches, he sat
down and told me he would wait there. McDonald's has an
armed guard outside its doors, and one of his functions is
to keep out street kids like Pedro. I wasn't happy to learn
that fact, but I made Pedro promise to wait right there.

I completely confess that I felt like the newly
crowned Social Service Queen of Latin America as I went
into McDonald's. I should have known better, but the full-
ness of the moment blinded me to what I know about the
way God works. I fully believe that God's favorite device is
irony, and in a few minutes God would remind me of that.

I had forgotten completely that Happy Meals come
with a toy, and I put the plastic Snoopy doll into my bag
because it didn't fit in the box. I returned to the park and
found Pedro waiting as promised. I said, "Pedro! Here is
your cheeseburger, your French fries, your Coca-Cola!"
Pedro reached out to take the food and drinks, but his face

*was still. I wondered what I could do to get the reaction I
was looking for, and then I remembered the toy in my bag.*

*"And look, Pedro, a Snoopy toy!" I pulled the doll
out of my bag and handed it to him. The moment when I
handed him the Snoopy and saw the look on his face was
a defining moment for me, both in my trip and within my
life. For all my posturing and my pride for buying Pedro
his meal—and certainly, I was providing him with a useful service—it was not me, nor the goods I provided, that
brought him joy.*

No, I was trumped by a plastic Snoopy toy.

*I relive the look on Pedro's face and the feeling in
my crushed heart every time I tell this story. I am reminded that no matter how great I think I am, no matter how
proud I am of myself for following Jesus in the way I see
fit, no matter how many miles I was from home, God was
right there with me, reminding me what it means to serve.*

*In that moment, in seeing unbrushed teeth spar-
kle in the presence of plastic Snoopy, I saw that service
doesn't have to be bought. The blessing is that God
works through us; through our pride, through our money,
through whatever lame earthly goal we have in mind. The
way of the kingdom is not the way of this earth.*

*I took Pedro's smile and lesson with me for the next
two and a half months I lived in Guatemala. I was careful when sharing my bounty of goods, but tried to give
in spirit abundantly. I kept looking for God every hour I
was there, and I was pleasantly surprised to continually
discover God was there. Whether God came in the form
of a child's dirty hands patting my white skin or in the joy
of having my friends land on the beach of San Juan on
the final Saturday of my trip, God was there. Serving me,
forming me, and leading me to do the same.*

I spent the majority of my time in San Juan. Solomon's Porch has included them in our community for eleven years now. We make the trek down there every spring to build homes for some of the poorest people in the village. Since the aforementioned trip of 2002 (the one I first attended), we as a church have been deliberate about having a presence of our community within theirs. In the fall of 2002, Shana Andersen began the intensive by including San Juan in her four-month stay in Guatemala. I was the winter 2003 addition, and after another Porch trip, Dustin Smith remained in San Juan for three weeks.

We live there not to provide a service (remember: you will be trumped by a plastic doll) but to continue to build friendships within the Body of Christ. It is truly a friendship and not just glorified visiting. All of us who have stayed in San Juan or returned are asked for updates on the absent. I found it a great honor to describe myself to those I had never met as Shana's friend, as Anna's friend, as a friend of Timiteo and Douglas El Gigante, as una miembra del Portico de Solomon. If we are not the company we keep—whether it's Jesus or simply our friends on earth, who are we? I am so blessed, as are many others of Solomon's Porch, to get to call many of the Guatemaltecos of San Juan La Laguna my friends.

SHAPED BY SERVICE

We recognize there's nothing original about sending people to build houses in Guatemala, giving money to people in need, or believing that serving others is an essential component of walking in the way of Jesus. We are not bushwhacking our way into new territory with some novel expression of Christianity. We are trying to ride along the rails of the well-established faith of those who have gone before us. And frankly, that's fine. Our motivation for serving others is not to be unique or hip.

We're committed to living lives of service because of its formative qualities. And that's where I think maybe there's something special going on. Service isn't something we do as a way of acting out our spirituality; it's a means through which our spirituality is shaped.

As I mentioned in Chapter 2, in the early days of Solomon's Porch, we were captured by a section from the book of James that reads, "Religion that God our Father accepts as pure and faultless is this: to look after orphans and widows in their distress and to keep oneself from being polluted by the world" (James 1:27).

We were enraptured by this call not as a way to live out our faith but as a means into our faith. As part of our spiritual formation, we wanted to answer that call and be useful religious people. We were then, and are still, quite sure that the world is not made better by more people having the "I'm not religious, I have a relationship with God" attitude. The world needs people who are living religiously useful lives in and for the world, and we wanted to be that kind of people. And we knew that we would not become such a people if we did not make service a normal practice of our spiritual formation.

Service is an obvious way for us to orient our lives around both a belief in Jesus and our efforts to live in the kingdom of God and never separate the two or pit them against each other. Living in the way of Jesus is not a result of a deeper devotion to the things of Jesus. It is what develops in us that deeper devotion.

One of the ways we describe ourselves is as a Holistic Missional Christian Community. It is a phrase that people read with a certain level of intrigue and a bit of confusion. As people are trying to figure out what that all means they will often say, "Is missional really a word?" (And it is. It is an adjective of the word mission.) There is something useful in using a peculiar word to describe ourselves because it causes people to think about what we're up to.

But there's more to it than a desire to be provocative. When we say we are a missional community, we are saying that we are not the end users of the gospel. Our belief in God and our orientation around the ways of Jesus is not for our benefit alone. Rather, we receive it so that we may be equipped and sent into the world to love our neighbors and serve "the least of these." In this sense, Solomon's Porch doesn't have a mission; it is missional.

Service is often seen primarily as a way in which the well-resourced reach out to others. But that perspective makes service feel like little more than drops of mercy bestowed upon the "needy" by those who are "blessed," rather than expressions of our desire to draw others into the kind of life where together we work toward making things on earth as they are in heaven.

Carol is a single mother with an eight-year-old son, Donald. For about a year, she lived in a house owned and subsidized by our church. When the time came for us to sell the house, she and Donald needed a place to live. For several months, members of our community used their connections with apartment managers, social workers, housing authorities, and job training services to help Carol find a safe, affordable place to live.

What was amazing to watch during this process, and during so many other times when our community has worked together to help someone, is that no one thought of Carol as a project. We were not doing these things as a veiled program attempt to try to get her to become a better Christian, although we recognize that our efforts contribute to Carol's understanding of what it means to live a life of faith. We weren't trying to be missionaries but friends who love and serve one another when there is a need.

The process of helping Carol find a home, or helping an unemployed mother get some furniture, or lending the van to a family with young children, not only benefits those individuals but also changes our community. When we participate in acts of service, we are stretching our faith to make sure it fits the world we live in. If our faith can't move us to feed someone who is hungry or help a single mother find shelter, it's simply not useful in the world.

THE NEIGHBORHOOD

There is something awesome in the call of the gospel to love our neighbors. This is not a mere suggestion; it is a requirement of those who are living in the way of Jesus. Toward this end, we are seeking to have a relationship with the world that is not "market driven." We are trying to avoid seeing service as a way of convincing people that the gospel is attractive. We are hopeful that our role in the world is not limited to teaching about God, or filling the felt needs of an ever-desiring culture, but one in which we love God and our neighbors without having ulterior motives for either of them. We are trying to have a posture of being good neighbors who are formed by the love of God and invite others into that process.

After our start in the upscale Linden Hills neighborhood, we moved into a neighborhood that is its socio-economic opposite. When we moved into our warehouse space, we experienced a wonderful, unexpected surprise. We discovered that two-thirds of our neighborhood didn't speak English as their first language, which meant they weren't likely to attend our worship gatherings. So we had to consider a posture with our neighbors that did not include their becoming "normal" participants at Solomon's Porch. That was the surprise. We had to consider how and why we love our neighbors as ourselves when the result will not increase the size of our church.

In addition, as a community, we had no interest in seeing ourselves as "urban commando Christians" doing the hard work of faith with the poor and needy; we wanted to love our neighbors. We did not target our neighborhood; circumstances, size, price, and availability made that building the clear choice for us. We did not see moving into the heart of the urban setting as a higher calling that cannot be matched by the suburban or rural contexts. It was the situation God orchestrated for us and we wanted to live into it.

We had very few models to look at in this effort. We didn't know of many young, thriving churches that moved from desirable neighborhoods into poor urban centers. We knew of those who had started in these situations and stayed, and even more that had moved out of them. Much of how we were trying to live in that neighborhood was the result of trial and error.

We wanted to have authentic friendships with our neighborhood. When we moved in, we took great care to not come with the attitude that we were going to "save the neighborhood" or "bring light to this dark place." Not only did that attitude feel like it had racial overtones, but it was not accurate. There were already many churches in our neighborhood and it is one of the most socially serviced neighborhoods in the country.

We were not bringing in that which was missing; we were invited to be the newest participants in the kingdom of God as it was unfolding on 13th Avenue in 2003. Our opportunity was to join in what was already going on and to be formed by joining in the work of "loving the least of these" just as we were being loved by them.

In order to keep our commitment to be a good neighbor, we decided that for the first year we would not have any formal involvement in the neighborhood. Instead, we wanted to learn what others were doing and how we could join them. We were more interested in being formed as people who are reconciled with God and the world than being people who provided program solutions.

We concentrated our efforts in that first year on being a welcoming presence, a friendly neighbor. It felt natural to ask neighborhood children to garden with us, to invite people to join us for our Sunday afternoon cookouts, and hold an open house so we could meet the neighbors.

We were not stagnant in our ministry during that first year. We met people from the neighborhood and many of them joined us in all kinds of kingdom-of-God efforts. But there was something healing about not having to create a series of programs to justify our existence. We had the chance to live and love as neighbors. We were concerned about being a disruption with all the cars coming into the neighborhood on Sunday nights, but we heard far more expressions of thanks than complaint. This good will might be as much a result of our keeping the front of the building clean and well-groomed as anything else. Or it could be that we share our cookouts with our neighbors at our cost and not theirs. But whatever the reason, for the most part they are as glad to be neighbors as we are.

After that first year, we felt like we could move into being more deliberate with our presence on the block. But even this had a bit of a twist on it. We didn't do research to see what the neighborhood needed and then create programs to meet those needs. Instead, we tried to impress on our people the practice of using whatever they had— ideas, passions, resources, abilities—for the work of the kingdom.

For us, serving our neighbors looks more like a guy lending out his lawnmower than a sophisticated social-service program. We created an Internet café that was available for our neighbors to use at no cost.

We had a facility that not only allowed space for our meetings but also served well as a room for a tutoring program for elementary-age children and a partnership with a group that taught English to Somali immigrants. We shared our space with another church that met on Saturday nights and with a group that helped teenage girls develop personal and job skills by making T-shirts. We restructured part of our facility to create a community laundry room. Because we have people who love children and are gifted at running camps, we developed a series of summer day camps with an emphasis on sports, art, and creativity.

Living as good neighbors is not always easy. In that neighborhood it wasn't always natural to take the time to meet the people on our street or behind our building because the language barrier was difficult to navigate. There was a fear of getting sucked into hard situations. But when we took the step to engage our lives with those around us and tried not only to think like Jesus but also to live like Jesus, we were transformed.

This posture didn't start with our move to that location. We were just as committed to being good neighbors in Linden Hills, where the needs were not necessarily financial or physical in nature. We helped staff a neighborhood festival. We'd walk around the nearby lake to pick up garbage. We ran an afternoon story time for children during the summer. These were modest attempts to figure out how to arrange our lives in a way that is in harmony with the things of God. We have recently partnered with a home in our neighborhood where three men and one woman who are suffering from the effects of the AIDS virus are supported as they deal with the dementia and other issues related to long-term exposure to AIDS medication.

Our strong desire to be a people who love and bless the world means we understand that service extends

WE ARE NOT ELIMINATING AIDS EVERYWHERE IN THE WORLD, BUT NOW AIDS IS PART OF OUR COMMUNITY. WE CAN'T IGNORE IT BECAUSE WE ARE CONNECTED TO IT.

beyond our threshold in both directions; we seek to care for those within our community with the same compassion we try to extend to those outside of our community. While we never want to back down from Jesus' call to serve the poor, we also recognize that there are many ways in which people are poor—the poor in spirit need the help of others as surely as those who are just plain poor.

We have helped people in our community pay rent, find a therapist, find a job, get medication, heal their marriages, deal with their divorces, treat their depression, find safe housing, and none of this has come through a structured program. This way of living is more than an outgrowth of our faith. It is essential to our life of connectedness.

INVENTIVE-AGE NEIGHBORS

To sum up the Good Samaritan story, our neighbor is anyone who needs our help, and living in the way of Jesus means freely giving that help. But this desire to be a good neighbor gets complicated in the Inventive Age. When the extent of a person's world was the distance they could walk in a day, it was easy to seek to live a reconciled life with your neighbors.

We live in a time when the stories of what is happening around the world are more accessible than the stories from our very own neighborhoods. It is not at all unusual for me to know details about what's going on in the Middle East before I know what's happening on Lake Street, even while I'm driving on Lake Street.

For the bulk of human history, people never saw the faces or heard the voices of those living on the other side of the planet. In the day of Jesus, it was common for people to not travel more than one hundred miles from their homes—Jesus probably didn't. When a person was called to care for the world, their "world" was really quite small. They didn't have to be concerned about people 10,000 miles away because they didn't even know there were people 10,000 miles away. But I do know it and that fundamentally changes the question of "Who is my neighbor?"

We go to bed every night knowing there are people all over the world for whom we are doing nothing. It's almost overwhelming to live out the call of Jesus to love our neighbor as ourselves when the world is our neighbor.

When we understand that the gospel is not for our use alone but for the benefit of the world, we can't avoid questions like, "What am I going to do about AIDS in Africa, war in the Middle East, and homelessness in Central

America?" When your neighbor is defined as anyone you have the opportunity to help, and you know of millions of people who need that help, it can be debilitating. But we are called to try.

There is a need to re-imagine the gospel's call on those of us who have the means to travel and connect with people anywhere in the world. The work of God in the world isn't reserved for long-term missionaries or Christian leaders. Today regular people can build housing developments and hospitals. We can arrange for food to feed an entire village or work toward freeing slaves. We can send artists and mothers and computer programmers to build homes in Guatemala. In 2011, my nineteen-year-old son Ruben moved to Guatemala to work in an orphanage. The day Ruben left, he said he wasn't nervous because of his two previous trips to Guatemala. He told me, "It isn't that different from here." The "other" had become part of him.

There are few, if any, excuses for us not to take our call to serve our global neighborhood.

Our desire to be a people who, as one of our dreams puts it, "are connected to, dependent on, and serve the global church" has led us to give resources to people in our community who travel to other parts of the world, to fund homes for AIDS orphans in India and Africa, to look into ministry opportunities in Jamaica, Africa, China, Iraq, and Afghanistan.

There are people who wonder why we make such an effort to be involved with the needy in places around the world when there is so much need in our own country. Our answer is simple: We see ourselves as members of the community of God and are not limited by our national allegiances. We are no less obligated to people who live in the borders of another country than we are to people who live inside our borders.

As people of the kingdom of God, we are called to serve the needy wherever and whenever we have the opportunity. We are interested in serving those in need regardless of where they live. In the integration mindset of the Inventive Age, borders, boundaries, and categories don't mean much.

How we care for the needy in the world is not something we've figured out, and we know our efforts to this point have been very limited. But we are quite sure that our faith must play out in a global way as well as a local way, and our formation as people living in harmony with God depends on it.

THE WORLD'S NOT OVER

Love them more than you wanted to
Love them more than you planned to
Love them when you don't feel it
Love them when you don't believe in it
Love them when you're numb.
Love them when you've run out of answers.

Oh the world's not over
Though darkness throws its shade
So bring your lamps right over
The dark won't rule the day.

Is there a time to kneel
A time to heal
A time to eat with one another?
A time to be
A time to see
To free a slave?

Is there a time to pray
A time to say
To cry out to our Mother?
Is there a time to be an angel's aid?

Oh the world's not over
Though darkness throws its shade
So bring your lamps right over
The dark won't rule the day.
And Jesus is the way,
Yes, Jesus is the way.

Is there a time to kneel
A time to heal
A time to eat with one another?
A time to be
A time to see
To free a slave?

Is there a time to pray
A time to say
To cry out to our Mother?
Is there a time to be an angel's aid?

Oh the world's not over
Though darkness throws its shade
So bring your lamps right over
The dark won't rule the day.
And Jesus is the way,
Yes, Jesus is the way.

—Cory Carlson

CHAPTER 12
OWNERSHIP AND
RESPONSIBILITY

Of the many questions I'm asked about our church and our attempts at being a community in the Inventive Age, the most common is something like, "Do you think what you're doing is the part of an emerging trend that others will chose to follow in the future?" Others get right to the point, asking, "Do you really think this is sustainable?" They think of what we're doing as trendy, as a reaction against the church that will experience its own backlash in time. They will press a bit deeper and ask if what we are doing is viable from a financial or church growth standpoint.

When I'm asked these questions, I answer, "I don't know, and it really doesn't matter that much to me." Validation of what we're attempting does not come from its attractiveness to others or its ability to last for generations. I am becoming more convinced that the real value of our efforts is found in our willingness to experiment and try. It's not important to me whether someone is still singing our songs or using our couches 15 years from now. It's the spirit of exploring, of seeking, of risking that I hope is inspiring to future generations to sense their responsibility to the world in which they live.

While we are committed to being led by the broader community of faith, including those who have come before us, we need to be people of the future. The church is called to be a people who are creating ways of spiritual formation and life with God that can flex and grow to meet the needs of the Inventive Age. If this kind of adaptability is necessary in our wardrobe, means of transportation, and medical practices, how much more important is it to our means of developing our faith? It is simply not consistent with the call of Christ to rely solely on the past for our ideas about community.

People sometimes get tripped up on this idea of thinking ahead because it sounds like I'm suggesting that we let the culture shape the church, which raises the "slippery slope" flag for some. So let me explain it like this. Shelley and I recently had a conversation about buying furniture for our home. We don't want to spend an excessive amount of money, but we want to buy good quality products. I mentioned to Shelley that I get tired of hearing people bemoan the "fact" that furniture makers don't make good, solid, well-crafted furniture anymore. I simply don't think that's true. There is plenty of finely made, high-quality furniture out there today as there ever was, but now it seems expensive because we have more access to cheaper products than during previous times.

We could buy a hand-crafted rocker or an armoire that will last for generations, but it will cost us. It's hard to swallow the expense when we know we could buy a cheaper, nice-enough version for a third of the price. So the struggle is not finding good quality furniture, it's being willing to pay for it. We asked ourselves if we wanted to be the kind of people who purchase high-quality goods so that our grandchildren will want to have our furniture or the kind who only live off the quality of generations gone by and buy cheap stuff made during our time.

In some ways, this is the question that needs to be asked by communities of faith as well. Will we do the hard and costly work of hand-crafting faith, or will we be content living off the antiques of previous generations and fill in with cheap imitations to "freshen up" the old stuff?

ARE WE WILLING TO BECOME THE ARTISANS OF NEW EXPRESSIONS OF FAITH THAT OUR GRANDCHILDREN WILL SEE AS A CONTINUATION OF ALL THE QUALITY THAT CAME BEFORE US?

Will they be therefore stirred to craft still newer, even more beautiful, more meaningful expressions of their own?

This book has been primarily about our efforts to live as a community of faith in the Inventive Age. But the creativity required to live an imaginative, experimental faith is not limited to what we do during our Sunday night gatherings or Wednesday night dinners. Central to the community life discussed in this book is the need for us—by which I mean not only our Solomon's Porch community but the church as a whole—to become theological communities. Toward this end, I suggest an understanding of theology as people of particular communities who hold certain beliefs that are played out in specific practices.

The work of theology must happen in full community and include the ideas of those who have come before us, but to simply accept the work of others as the end of the conversation, to outsource the "real" thinking to scholars from another time or place, turns theology into a stagnant philosophy rather than an active study of how we are to live God's story in our time.

The kinds of communities that will be best equipped for the task of spiritual formation in the Inventive Age will be those who take ownership of and responsibility for the practice of theology as an essential element of their lives together. This is in no way a call to be less theological, but for our communities to be more involved in the work of theology as a necessary part of the spiritual formation process.

Wouldn't it be wonderful if the task of both the new convert to Christianity and the experienced Christian were understood as not only believing the things of Christianity, but as the need to contextualize, create, articulate, and live the expressions of faith in their world?

I don't see this vision as an indictment against the contemporary church as much as a dream that fits in with the way the Christian church has always modified its methods to meet the needs of the body. The church has certainly been in similar places before and will undoubtedly end up there again; it is one of the great stories of church history that followers of Jesus base their attempts at ministry and life on the thinking of days gone by, only to see those efforts fail miserably. It's that failure that often leads to transition.

New Testament Christians certainly had their version of this story with the debate surrounding how non-

Jews would be called to live as followers of Jesus. The discussion involved whether they would need to adopt the Jewish way of faith or if they could express Christianity as non-Jews. I am confident that just as the early Christians found their way to a kind of spiritual formation that allowed Gentiles to fully follow Jesus in culturally appropriate ways, we too will gradually move beyond the approaches of spiritual formation that are remnants of eras past to one more fitting to the time we live in.

We are invited to live a faith like that of Abram. We are called into new lands, with new ways of living. We are called to be radically committed to an unknown future. We can only sustain that commitment with the faith that God goes with us. The future of the church does not rest in finding new ways to do the same old things; it is finding new ways to do the new things of Jesus in this age.

May you be blessed in all your ways.

GO IN PEACE

Go in peace
Seeking on
United bought and freed.
In times of trial
Our hopes should be
Spirit filled
And holy.

May you be
Eternally
Blessed and wonderfully

Led all your days
By love's pure light
Prayerful in all ways.
All ways.

Sow in peace
Dream of a place
Love in the name of the lord.
Stay in peace
May Christ surround you.
The kingdom of God has no end.

Amen. Amen. Amen. Amen.

—Ben Johnson

P.S.

We are seeking to be an Inventive Age church as an act of faithfulness, yet it's not necessarily intentional. We are Inventive Age people, so it makes sense that we would create an Inventive Age church.

I have tried to tell the story of our community as we are currently living. It might be that 575 weeks from now we will have changed so much that this book barely describes us. Frankly, I hope that's the case. I'm hopeful that we will stay in tune with what God is up to and that as new people join us they reshape us. I hope that we will not simply become a community with new people, but a community made new by those people.

And I hope that whatever impulses brought you to read this book will grow. I invite you and your community to engage with us, to help shape us as we help shape you. We invite you to join us, to message us, and mostly to inspire us. We trust that your community has much to show us.

So please share. www.SolomonsPorch.com and Facebook.com/SolomonsPorchPage.

Doug - on behalf of the Solomon's Porch Community

February 2011

START ANEW

He said, "Don't mind me, I'm at home with my sorrow"
You see all my lies they left with my friends.
Well is it hard waking up to tomorrow?
Is there something that won't let you go?

"What I've done has just made me hollow
It's only just that this be my end,
And you say that you can give
A new day
And erase my shame."

We can start anew
We can make it all up again
We can make it through
We can get it all unstuck again

In the blanks that are waiting for us
How you want your verse, your chorus to go?
On the voice of a fleet of angels
We were meant to be more than strangers—not alone.

So tell me how you want this thing to go
Cause dreams don't die and you're not on your own.

We can start anew
We can make it all up again
We can make it through
We can get it all unstuck again

In the blanks that are waiting for us
How you want your verse, your chorus to go?
On the voice of a fleet of angels
We were meant to be more than strangers—not alone.

So tell me how you want this thing to go
Cause dreams don't die and you're not on your own.

You're not alone.

—Cory Carlson

ABOUT THE AUTHOR

Doug Pagitt is the founder of Solomon's Porch, a holistic missional Christian community in Minneapolis, Minnesota, and one of the pioneering leaders of Emergent Village, a social network of Christians around the world. He is also cofounder of an event and social media company and author of a number of groundbreaking books: *A Christianity Worth Believing, Church in the Inventive Age, and Preaching in the Inventive Age*.

Doug can be reached at:

Twitter: @Pagitt

www.DougPagitt.com

www.facebook.com/DougPagittspage

www.SolomonsPorch.com

CPSIA information can be obtained at www.ICGtesting.com
Printed in the USA
LVOW01s2036270614

392088LV00009B/62/P